Elements in Crime Narratives
edited by
Margot Douaihy
Emerson College
Catherine Nickerson
Emory College of Arts and Sciences
Henry Sutton
University of East Anglia

FEMALE ANGER IN CRIME FICTION

Caroline Reitz
John Jay College of Criminal Justice and the CUNY Graduate Center

Shaftesbury Road, Cambridge CB2 8EA, United Kingdom

One Liberty Plaza, 20th Floor, New York, NY 10006, USA

477 Williamstown Road, Port Melbourne, VIC 3207, Australia

314–321, 3rd Floor, Plot 3, Splendor Forum, Jasola District Centre, New Delhi – 110025, India

103 Penang Road, #05–06/07, Visioncrest Commercial, Singapore 238467

Cambridge University Press is part of Cambridge University Press & Assessment, a department of the University of Cambridge.

We share the University's mission to contribute to society through the pursuit of education, learning and research at the highest international levels of excellence.

www.cambridge.org
Information on this title: www.cambridge.org/9781009539333

DOI: 10.1017/9781009358699

© Caroline Reitz 2024

This publication is in copyright. Subject to statutory exception and to the provisions of relevant collective licensing agreements, no reproduction of any part may take place without the written permission of Cambridge University Press & Assessment.

When citing this work, please include a reference to the DOI 10.1017/9781009358699

First published 2024

A catalogue record for this publication is available from the British Library.

ISBN 978-1-009-53933-3 Hardback
ISBN 978-1-009-35867-5 Paperback
ISSN 2755-1873 (online)
ISSN 2755-1865 (print)

Cambridge University Press & Assessment has no responsibility for the persistence or accuracy of URLs for external or third-party internet websites referred to in this publication and does not guarantee that any content on such websites is, or will remain, accurate or appropriate.

Female Anger in Crime Fiction

Elements in Crime Narratives

DOI: 10.1017/9781009358699
First published online: December 2024

Caroline Reitz
John Jay College of Criminal Justice and the CUNY Graduate Center
Author for correspondence: Caroline Reitz, creitz@jjay.cuny.edu

Abstract: Feminist anger is having a moment, but the double meaning of "mad" as angry and crazy has shaped the representation of women in popular crime fiction since Lady Audley burned down the house over 150 years ago. But when is anger just, when is it revenge, and when is it maddening? This Element will explore the ethics and efficacy of anger in female-centered crime fiction from its first stirrings in the nineteenth century through second-wave feminism's angry, individualist heroes to today's current explosion of women who reject respectability and justification. It will also examine recent challenges to our understanding of the genre posed both by feminist care ethics and by intersectional crime fiction. This Element considers anger as the appropriate affect for women fighting for justice and explores how it shapes the representation of female detectives, relates to the crimes they investigate, and complicates ideas around justice.

Keywords: crime fiction, anger, women, justice, violence

© Caroline Reitz 2024

ISBNs: 9781009539333 (HB), 9781009358675 (PB), 9781009358699 (OC)
ISSNs: 2755-1873 (online), 2755-1865 (print)

Contents

1 Foreword   1

2 Mad?   13

3 Using It   25

4 Losing It   45

5 Epilogue   61

   References   64

1 Foreword

It was 2018 in Trump's America, with the repeal of *Roe* v. *Wade* and the current wave of anti-LGBTQIA+ laws still in the future. I'd been reading, watching, and teaching female-centered crime narratives for the past thirty years, stories full of angry women, ranging from clear-eyed justice-seekers to self-destructive femme fatales.[1] But very little of my crime fiction nous helped me make sense of *Killing Eve*, a BBC series that debuted in 2018, featuring a global cat-and-mouse game between three women: an MI5 agent, an MI6 agent, and a psychopathic assassin. The show, based on a series of novellas by Luke Jennings, and helmed by a different female showrunner each season, is both violent and stylish, horrific and hilarious. It seemed to know, flaunt, and undermine all the rules of representing women in crime narrative.[2] While the genre of crime narrative is broad, as with any genre, there are conventions that shape our expectations.[3] As Lauren Berlant writes in *The Female Complaint*, "a genre is an aesthetic structure of affective experience, an institution or formation that absorbs all kinds of small variations or modifications while promising that the persons transacting with it will experience the pleasure of encountering what they expected" (Berlant 2008: 4). When transacting with crime narratives, even my most cynical self expects some kind of justice. *Killing Eve* dispensed with any of it: Who do you root for? Could this story have a moral? Could it possibly be a feminist moral? I hadn't been this confused since 1991, weeping as Thelma and Louise flew their convertible to certain death while my fellow theatergoers cheered.[4] *Killing Eve* recklessly plays with expectations around the boundaries between female anger and insanity, toying with the "crazy bitch" trope long used to dismiss the legitimacy of women's emotions. I had just finished watching the seventh season of *Homeland*, with its angry, bipolar female spy. My syllabus in the following years would include Natsuo Kirino's *Out* (1997; translated 2003), Oyinkan Braithwaite's *My Sister, the Serial Killer*

---

[1] I use the term "female-centered crime narrative" to represent works that center female characters and experience. The vast majority of works here are written by authors who identify as female.

[2] The showrunners for the four seasons of *Killing Eve* were Phoebe Waller-Bridge (2018), Emerald Fennell (2019), Suzanne Heathcoate (2020), and Laura Neal (2022).

[3] See Cathy Cole's *Private Dicks and Feisty Chicks: An Interrogation of Crime Fiction*, especially the first chapter, where she suggests that "writing about crime fiction entails defining and interrogating a genre which, like an uncooperative suspect, resists questioning" (Cole 2004: 10). What I call "crime narrative" includes fiction, television, and film, and, for all its variety, retains "its capacity to remain readable or audible across the field of all its variations" (Berlant 2008: 4).

[4] See Rita Felski's chapter "Identifying with Characters" in *Character: Three Inquiries in Literary Studies* (Anderson, Felski, & Moi 2019) for an analysis of complicated "collective identification" with the doomed characters in *Thelma and Louise*.

(2018), and Ottessa Moshfegh's *Eileen* (2015).[5] Madness and anger have long held hands in female-centered crime narrative, but something new seemed to be going on.

Or maybe we were just back where we started, in the messy sensation fiction of the 1860s.[6] In Mary Elizabeth Braddon's *Lady Audley's Secret* (1987 [1862]), a wronged woman goes very wrong, solving her problems with (attempted) murder and arson. Feminists have debated her righteous anger or murderous madness almost ever since, most memorably in Elaine Showalter's second-wave roar: "Lady Audley's real secret is that she is *sane*, and, moreover, representative" (Showalter 1977: 167). But the clarity of that call has dissipated. The election of Trump in 2016 was an inflection point in the conversation about gender, anger, and justice, most pronouncedly in the US, but with reverberations around the world. Here is just a sample of the works written about female anger in the years following Trump's election, all of which contribute to my observations: Soraya Chemaly's *Rage Becomes Her: The Power of Women's Anger*, Myesha Cherry's *The Case for Rage: Why Anger is Essential to Anti-Racist Struggle*, Brittney Cooper's *Eloquent Rage: A Black Feminist Discovers Her Superpower*, Carol Gilligan's *Why Does Patriarchy Persist* (with Naomi Snider) and *Darkness Made Visible: Patriarchy's Resurgence and Feminist Resistance* (with David A. J. Richards), Kate Manne's *Down Girl: The Logic of Misogyny*, Laurie Penny's *Bitch Doctrine*, and Rebecca Traister's *Good and Mad: The Revolutionary Power of Women's Anger*.[7] If Trump's election was a primal scene of white-supremacist capitalist hetero-patriarchy (to use bell hooks's entirely apt term), then these works constitute a primal scream.

While anger in female-centered crime narrative is and has been about many things, it is clear today that women are angry about the precarity of justice in a world in which women "compose 70 percent of victims killed by an intimate partner" (Burke & Clarke 2021: 6).[8] The explosion of the True Crime genre has been connected to a loss of faith in the ability of the criminal legal system to

---

[5] The primary and secondary sources I use in my classes and in this Element are drawn from the Anglosphere, for the obvious reasons of my own English-language limitations, but also because of the outsize role English has played in the critical conversation around crime fiction. This is changing, as both crime fiction and scholarship outside the Anglosphere are recognized as shaping the field and altering our sense of literary history; see Stewart King (2014). While most of my texts were written originally in English, I discuss two in translation: *Out* and Gu Byeong-Mo's *The Old Woman with the Knife*.

[6] Peters (2018).

[7] And the list goes on: Since first writing this manuscript, I now have Elizabeth Flock's *The Furies: Women, Vengeance, and Justice* (2024) and Victoria Smith's *Hags: The Demonisation of Middle-Aged Women* (2023) on my desk.

[8] When this Element uses the words "female" and "woman," it means people who identify as women.

render justice. A significant majority of the consumers of True Crime, often featuring graphic descriptions of female victims, are women.[9] It is also true that 47 percent of white women voted for Trump, and that we tend especially to follow crimes in which the victims are young, pretty, and white.[10] Women are complicated. And even if feminist anger at patriarchal injustice seems straightforward, anger is complicated. Alison Jagger explores the "epistemological privilege" of anger (Jagger 1989). Brittney Cooper explains that the costs of rage "are directly proportional to the amount of power any given woman or girl has when she chooses to wield it" (Cooper 2018: 167). From the stereotype of the Angry Black Woman and its roots in "misogynoir" to the many ways that anger disguises itself, women's multiple social positions and varying cultural backgrounds compound and complicate the expression of anger.[11] But while emotions are messy, the role historically played by Black and working-class writers in demanding more from our anger is clear. Just as Black women, such as Stacey Abrams and Fani Willis in Georgia and Letitia James in New York, have been at the center of the political resistance to Trump, Black women writers have kept us focused on anger's connection to justice from the genre's first stirrings in Pauline E. Hopkins's *Hagar's Daughter* (2021a). Section 1.1 presents a theoretical frame around gender, anger, and justice, drawing from multiple understandings of how female anger has been and continues to be understood, and from arguments about crime narrative's representation of this experience. Section 1.2 provides a brief overview of the sections that follow.

1.1 Structures of Seething: Gender, Anger, and Justice

What is the proper affect for justice in female-centered crime narratives? Anger seems like an obvious answer. Many theorists of anger begin with Aristotle's *Nicomachean Ethics*: "the man who is angry at the right things and with the right people ... is praised" (quoted in Fisher 2002: 173). Myisha Cherry writes that "long before philosophers like me were born," philosophers understood "anger's uses for preventing injustice and pursuing justice" (Cherry 2021: 62). But as Sianne Ngai explains in *Ugly Feelings*, "while numerous thinkers have

---

[9] See Cruz 2015; Burke 2021b. See also Laura Browder, who explores female readers' allegiance to True Crime as a mechanism for coping with patriarchal violence (Browder 2006).

[10] The figure is often given as 52 percent, but that was based on less reliable exit polling. See Molly Ball's October 2018 article in *Time* magazine: "Donald Trump Didn't Really Win 52% of White Women in 2016" (https://time.com/5422644/trump-white-women-2016/). Gwen Ifill coined the term "Missing White Woman Syndrome" to explain the disproportionate attention given to white female victims of crime; see https://bit.ly/3JvEH5s). Lenika Cruz (2015) asks "when was the last time the victim in a true-crime story was a young unarmed black man?"

[11] Moya Bailey coined the term "misogynoir" to describe the intersection between misogyny and anti-Black racism (see, e.g., Bailey 2021).

valued anger for its connections to justice, its *justifiability* seems always in question" (Ngai 2005: 182). Or, as Cooper puts it, "owning anger is a dangerous thing" (Cooper 2018: 2). If female anger has, in the words of Anna Bogutskaya, a "toxic unruliness," how do we get the power of disruption necessary for justice without the toxicity (Bogustskaya 2023: 131)? In other words, can we use anger without losing it? Crime writer Megan Abbott, in a 2018 interview, explains that there is

> a lot of rage on all sides that have bubbled to the surface. I think the moment for women's crime fiction is going to last a lot longer than it might have otherwise but then again could it have arrived at any other time? As with everything in literature, something is present before it is quite articulated, and then someone identifies it, gives it a name, and the unconscious becomes conscious.

One way of envisioning this unruly, not-quite-articulated rage is "structures of seething." Riffing on Raymond Williams's concept of "structures of feeling," "structures of seething" allow us to think about a female anger made messy by the many different problems and possibilities contained in and expressed by this rage. Introduced in Williams's 1954 *Preface to Film* and developed in his 1961 *The Long Revolution* (and elsewhere), "structures of feeling" denotes the interplay between the tangible and intangible aspects of the culture of a period, both the visible surface and those unconscious aspects bubbling underneath and, occasionally, up. Williams suggests that structures of feeling register "evidence of the deadlocks and unsolved problems of the society," that are "often admitted to consciousness for the first time" in ephemeral popular culture (Williams 1961: 48). Tangible things, like published literature, can show up in an archive and tell a particular story about the culture and, in Williams's words, its "public ideals," such as justice or democracy. But Williams understands that the canonical texts that tend to stand in for various historical moments do not fully capture "structures of feeling." I suspect readers of Elements in Crime Narratives would concur. Williams's framework holds space for the "intangible," what he knows is there but can't be seen. He understands that art reflects "public ideals," such as justice, as well as the "omissions" from those public ideals, such as injustice struggling to become visible (Williams 1961: 63). Denise Mina agrees. Writing recently about her deal with the Raymond Chandler estate to write three new Philip Marlowe novels, she argues that commercial crime fiction's ability to "mirror a moment ... potentially imperils a book's longevity" but also provides "the chance to change the way we speak collectively about a moment and become a powerful driver of social change" (Mina 2023).

Being left out of public ideals, such as equal representation under the law, is part of why women are mad as hell. It is not just women; we live in an angry time.¹² In the US, from contested election results to insurrections and mass shootings, it is impossible to ignore male anger. The expression of female anger is traditionally less visible. As Sara Robinson explains, "Women's rage has been so sublimated for so long that there's simply no frame for what happens when it finally comes to the surface" (quoted in Traister 2018: 241). "Structures of seething" is the frame I've chosen because it apprehends several key aspects of the history, experience, and representation of female anger and attempts to make anger's messiness more legible without requiring clarity or closure, as previous theories of anger have done. "Structures of seething" connote anger's connection to structural violence and power, though, as we will see, one way structural violence functions is by individualizing anger. The use of *structures* indicates that, as Kimberlé Crenshaw has taught us, there are multiple forces that compound to shape an individual's access both to her anger and to justice.¹³ A "structure" suggests regulation and containment, as does "seething": one is always "quietly seething."¹⁴ Seething also then suggests a sense of waiting, of biding one's time, which contains the possibility of, to use Sara Ahmed's formulation, a "feminist snap." A snap is "a quick, sudden movement," but, Ahmed explains, it is "only the start of something because of what we do not notice ... When a snap is registered as the origin of violence, the one who snaps is deemed violent" (Ahmed 2017: 189). Today's violent antihero is less the swaggering hard-boiled sleuth who fights for justice by her own rules with some questionable choices (such as Kate Winslett's Mare in the 2021 TV show *Mare of Easttown*), and more one who has abandoned "public ideals" altogether. As Sarah Hagelin and Gillian Silverman note about today's television antiheroes, women increasingly "want raw naked power ... or even worse, absolutely nothing" (Hagelin & Silverman 2022: xii). We have seen this coming, from the rise of domestic noir to rape-revenge stories like Emerald Fennell's *Promising Young Woman*, from Lisbeth Salander in the *Millenium Trilogy* to June/Offred in the *Handmaid's Tale*, to the often inscrutable texts on my syllabus.¹⁵

---

[12] See Robinson (2023), in which he considers recent feminist writings on anger as well as the question of right-wing anger. A much-reviewed recent work, Pankaj Mishra's *Age of Anger: A History of the Present* (Farrar Straus Giroux, 2017), provides only a cursory consideration of women's anger.

[13] Crenshaw (1991).

[14] In thinking about affective structures, I have been influenced by Manne's *Down Girl* and her understanding of misogyny as a "*systematic* social phenomenon" that thinks about misogyny in terms of "what it *does* to women" as well as what ideologies it upholds and how its "mechanisms of enforcement vary widely, depending on the overall social position of differently situated girls and women" (Manne 2018: 21, 13).

[15] Bogutskaya has an extended reading of *Promising Young Woman* and its demand that we look "directly into an ugly kernel of anger that is both righteous and self-destructive all at once" (Bogutskaya 2023: 130).

Is there a way out of this story somewhere in between compliance and dismemberment? Or is it time to realize that believing in justice has always been for women, to use Berlant's phrase, a "cruel optimism," a continued attachment to something that is hostile to one's flourishing. To be clear, actual justice would never be hostile to one's flourishing; the point here is that to continue to work for it without results (from the criminal legal system to crime narrative) might be.[16] As Rita Felski says about the detective story in *The Limits of Critique* (2015), when "matters of the law have very little to do with matters of justice" the critic "may prefer to side with the figure of the criminal" (Felski 2015: 101). *Killing Eve* demonstrates this truth; it also wonders, in this post-snap world, if it even matters if one is angry, insane, or so angry that you are driven insane.

But it does matter. There has been a long feminist and especially Black feminist tradition of arguing that anger is essential to the recognition of injustice. Audre Lorde wrote in "The Uses of Anger" that every "woman has a well-stocked arsenal of anger potentially useful against the oppressions, personal and institutional, which brought that anger into being. Focused with precision it can be a powerful source of energy serving progress and change" (Lorde 1981: 8). More recently, in *The Case for Rage*, Myesha Cherry argues that anger "makes us attentive to wrongdoing and motivates us to pursue justice" (Cherry 2021: 31). But she carefully distinguishes "Lordean rage" from other types of rages (such as "rogue rage" or "narcissistic rage") that can veer toward violence and chaos; indeed, the need for multiple categories for anger illustrates its unruly nature. Lorde herself qualifies that anger must be "focused with precision." Complicating matters further, if the focusing of women's angry feelings are key to justice, regulation of them is also instrumental to patriarchy.[17] As Soraya Chemaly explains, "abandoning our anger is a necessary adaptation to a perpetual undercurrent of possible male violence" (Chemaly 2018: xix). So when does regulation serve justice and when does it serve the status quo? That is a hard question to answer. The essays in bell hooks's *Killing Rage* suggest that anger, however righteous, can have a "maddening impact," blurring the line between madness and justifiable anger at, say, structural racism, homophobia, or patriarchy (hooks 1995: 23). Laurie Penny writes in *Bitch Doctrine* that rage might look different over time: "when resistance fails to produce relief... rage finds outlets wherever it can" (Penny 2018: 375). Carol Gilligan describes "protest" as a natural reaction to injustice, but "when protest proves ineffective ... despair and then detachment" follow (Gilligan & Snider 2018: 14).

---

[16] Marcie Bianco makes a similar argument about feminism and equality in her recent book *Breaking Free: The Lie of Equality and the Feminist Fight for Freedom* (2023).
[17] See Manne 2018.

This is all too unruly for Martha Nussbaum, who does not agree that anger is an effective vehicle for justice.[18] In *Anger and Forgiveness*, Nussbaum writes about the two stories of the Furies in Aeschylus's *Oresteia*: the familiar one of fury and violence, and the lesser known one of the incorporation of these mad women back into the social order. She writes, "unchanged these Furies could not be part and parcel of a working legal system in a society committed to the rule of law. You don't put wild dogs in a cage and come out with justice. But the Furies do not make the transition to democracy unchanged" (Nussbaum 2016: 2). Democracy requires a regulation of feeling: The Furies are transformed into "the Kindly Ones" and therefore allowed to be part of society.[19] Nussbaum is concerned that anger is always backward-looking, always about payback: It is too hard to use it and not to lose it. This position is not without merit. Oscar Schwartz, writing about #MeToo, explains that "call out culture" both "achieve-[s] social justice where traditional institutions fail to deliver it" and can also mete out "disproportionate and unregulated punishment" (Schwartz 2018). Clarity where anger is concerned is a big ask.

Crime fiction, despite the stereotype of an all-knowing Great Detective who wraps everything up in the final pages, is not a space of clarity. It is a place where cultural meanings get contested, where, pace Raymond Williams, we might catch a glimpse of our inchoate feelings. Part of anger's messiness is that it is sometimes not easily distinguishable from a range of other feelings that don't have its traditional connections with justice or action. Ngai writes about these "ugly feelings," characterizing irritation as "a conspicuously weak or inadequate form of anger" (Ngai 2005: 35). The feelings that Ngai considers, such as irritation and envy, are "*a*moral and *non*cathartic, offering no satisfactions of virtue, however oblique, nor any therapeutic or purifying release" (Ngai 2005: 6). Allison Pease, writing about boredom and Modernist women's writing, sees boredom as a "manifestation of repressed anger" (Pease 2012: 86). When women feel angry, it can not only look like other things – boredom, guilt, madness – but it can be hard even to know. "The taboos against our feeling and expressing anger are so powerful, that even *knowing* when we are angry is not a simple matter," explains Harriet Goldhor Lerner in *The Dance of Anger*,

---

[18] It's not just Nussbaum. The idea that justice would be tainted by emotion is built into our notion of justice as blind. Writing in *Why Does Patriarchy Persist*, Naomi Snider explains that in her legal training, "I was schooled in the need to separate reason from emotion and to hide vulnerability. I was taught that emotions – making things personal – polluted the pursuit of justice" (Gilligan & Snider 2018: 103).

[19] Gilligan and Richards call out the patriarchal logic of this move: "The argument for democracy is thus at the outset deeply flawed along gendered lines . . . . Athena enforces the patriarchal gender binary and hierarchy that elevate reason (masculine) over emotion (feminine) and force the suppression of women's anger in the name of rationality and kindness" (Gilligan & Richards 2018: 11).

a best-selling work of pop psychology first published in 1985 (Lerner 1985: 2). Sometimes angry women are represented as dissociated, or reject feelings altogether, represented in femme fatales as well the new crop of female assassins considered in the "Losing It" section. This uncertainty is captured in tropes like racial passing, which is at the heart of a few of the novels considered here.

"Structures of seething" apprehend anger's complex ecosystem, as womens' attempts to process messy feelings trouble the surface of female-centered crime narrative, like the Furies lurking beneath the Kindly Ones. Seething as a state indicates both anger and waiting, which introduces the problem of time. Time is an important element of all narrative, but it is particularly important to crime fiction. Both the crime itself, as well as the solution to the crime, have their own timelines on the road to resolution.[20] But time, too, is complicated, as crime narratives contain fuzzy flashbacks and unreliable narrators and witnesses, or explore trauma's effect on memory. Crime fiction most obviously values knowing, but it equally dramatizes not knowing. In *Contemporary Drift: Genre, Historicism, and the Problem of the Present*, Theodore Martin (2019) has theorized "waiting" as central to the detective story. Martin explains that waiting is not so much the time between not knowing and knowing (for example, the discovery of the body and then the identification of the killer), but as simultaneously knowing and not knowing. Martin argues that "the logic of the wait thus pivots on its axis. No longer pointing toward an anticipated future, the wait redirects our attention to the complexity of a present in crisis" (p. 105). Waiting allows us to see beyond the narrative dictates of the crime story, from the "anticipated future" of narrative closure or social justice to a present where we are in the process of trying to figure out what to do. Alice Walker's poem "To be a Woman" serves as an epigraph to Rebecca Traister's *Good and Mad*. The speaker reassures us that "The Feminine/Is not/Dead/Nor is she/Sleeping/Angry, yes,/Seething, yes./Biding her time;/Yes./Yes." Seething is anger contained, but it is also anger waiting. Liz Evans, writing about domestic noir, suggests something similar. "One way of reconceptualizing female aggression," she writes, "is to shift the focus away from the traditional masculine model of action toward one of capacity to act" (Evans 2021: 39). Thinking about action in terms of capacity, rather than action itself, affords some time to figure out how/if to use one's anger. It allows for a state of vigilance, as Ahmed discusses, distinguishing here between action and capacity: "vigilantism" is not only "taking the law

---

[20] Tzvetan Todorov's famous discussion of detective fiction in "The Typology of Detective Fiction" emphasizes the genre's double narrative: the story of the crime and the story of the investigation (Todorov 1977). See also Hamilton 2021 for her discussion of history, trauma, and detective fiction in Paretsky.

into your own hands (the law as rod is precisely what we are fighting against), but also as a feminist vigil, as a demand to stay awake to, or to wake up to, the violence directed against women" (Ahmed 2017: 208). The emphasis on capacity, however, could also look like action deferred. One of the recurring features of the female-centered crime narrative is that a particular crime is solved, but a different (or broader) crime is left unsolved. The narrative contains both resolution and unfinished business. As we will see, endings are muted, forced, sometimes performatively happy, sometimes, in the words of Philip Marlowe, with the sleuth becoming "part of the nastiness" (Chandler 1992, 230).

Some feminist theorists of justice, perhaps wary of "cruel optimism" or fearing the turn to violence, advocate care. "[G]enerosity and empathy," Nussbaum suggests, rather than anger, "help to construct a future of justice." Revolutionary leaders need to be "creatures of love," a quality that goes "well with the project of building something better than what exists already" (Nussbaum 2016: 8–9).[21] Since Carole Gilligan's *In A Different Voice*, an ethics grounded in care rather than justice is often seen as *the* feminist solution.[22] Maria Tatar, whose *The Heroine with 1,001 Faces* has chapters on both "Detective Work" and "Caring Detectives," argues for a "heroism that is driven less by empathy than by attentive care" (Tatar 2021: xx). Penny, writing in 2018 in response to continued assaults on social norms, explains that "we must navigate a course between the exhaustion of perpetual outrage and the numbness of normalisation. That means taking care of ourselves and of one another" (Penny 2018: 120). One model for this care is sisterhood and working in a community. We see this employed, explored, or, in bleaker works, explicitly rejected as a path to justice in nearly all the works discussed.

The rejection of sisterhood, as well as of love and community, underscores a problem long associated both with crime fiction and with white feminism: the commitment to individualism.[23] Individualism shares the same complications as anger: it embodies agency, as well as the capacity for action, but it can isolate and be self-destructive. Nevertheless, it is an obvious trait in a hero-centered genre.[24] As Tatar writes, "women sleuths ... tend to be loners" (Tatar 2021: 206). Regulating feelings, particularly anger, is tied to being a successful individual, whether that is a private detective, a cop on the force, or a having-it-all housewife. But it can atomize rather than bring us together; the angry woman is always an individual, Anna Bogutskaya writes, "never angry on behalf of other women, and there has definitely been little room for intersectional anger" (Bogutskaya 2023: 126). While this is not uniformly true of

---

[21] Cherry 2018: 49–65 argues that anger is compatible with goodwill and respect.
[22] Reitz 2015: 19–46; Nash 2001: 1–24.   [23] See Munt 1994, especially chapter 2.
[24] Reitz 1999: 213–233.

female-centered crime narratives, as we will see, it is true that patriarchy attempts to keep women angry about the wrong things, blaming individuals for systemic injustice (Gilligan & Snider 2018 : 66).[25] Cooper points out that "[n]eoliberalism is endlessly concerned with 'personal responsibility' and individual self-regulation" as a way to shift responsibility from systems to individuals (Cooper 2018: 122). Loner sleuths chasing deranged criminals, in Patricia Cornwell's novels, for example, can reinforce these cultural narratives.[26]

How might we turn anger to justice without some of the pitfalls noted earlier? What would be an effective affective practice for both acknowledging harm and moving toward justice? Judith Butler suggests mourning. Her writing post-9/11, another inflection point in thinking about justice, searches for a different kind of accountability for the violence that passes under the name of safeguarding democracy. In *Precarious Life: The Powers of Mourning and Violence*, Butler writes that "President Bush announced on September 21 that we have finished grieving and that *now* it is time for resolute action to take the place of grief." However, Butler continues that "when grieving is something to be feared, our fears can give rise to the impulse to resolve it quickly, to banish it in the name of an action invested with the power to restore the loss or return the world to a former order, or to reinvigorate a fantasy that the world formerly was orderly" (Butler 2004: 29–30). This facile move from chaos to restored order echoes a stereotypical promise of traditional crime fiction. Butler advocates mourning both because it slows things down and allows us to sit with our feelings, and because it demands that we pay attention to victims of violence, rather than aggressors; accountability is mourning's super power. We see a similar emphasis in feminist calls in crime fiction scholarship to pay more attention to victims and the conditions of vulnerability for women rather than to the perpetrator or scenes of pornographic violence. Cathy Cole's *Private Dicks and Feisty Chicks* considers the use of violence in feminist crime writing, noting that victims get repeatedly violated: by the writer, the killer, the investigator(s), and the readers themselves (Cole 2004: 102–108). Cole is also a crime novelist, and she explains that one "of the first challenges for feminist crime writers is to give

---

[25] Philip Fisher thinks such individualizing is a misunderstanding of Aristotelian anger: "The passions are incited ... by what happens not simply to myself but to parents, to those I love, to children, brothers, sisters, friends, neighbors – that is, to those who make up our world" (Fisher 2002: 173).

[26] See Cole on Cornwell (Cole, 2004: 217–219). Though this observation is beyond the scope of this Element, Chen 2005 makes the important point that problematizing the individual subject and her agency comes with poststructuralist baggage. "Poststructuralist conceptions of identity ... have been embraced in the academy at precisely a moment when minorities are claiming for themselves the right to speak as subjects and agents" (Chen, 2005: 192). An intersectional lens is crucial to understanding the shifting terrain of individual identity in female-centered crime narratives.

these victims a voice" (Cole 2004: 151).[27] Mourning victims of violence might accommodate anger without the risks of revenge, without always "kicking down" (Robinson 2023). Regulating, snapping, passing, ruminating, waiting, caring, mourning – these are all parts of the structures of seething, a way of keeping potentially unruly female anger both in view and in process. We will see them all explored in the sections that follow.

1.2 Mad? Using It. Losing It.

Three sections follow this Introduction. "Mad?" looks back at some defining angry woman, both perpetrators and sleuths, in nineteenth- and early twentieth-century crime narratives. A conversation about the relationship between madness and anger weaves in and out of these texts, one alive and well in today's domestic noir. A central text in this conversation, Mary Elizabeth Braddon's *Lady Audley's Secret* (1987 [1862]), illustrates how early crime stories begin to articulate how anger might – and might not – be used for justice in societies where women do not have full legal rights. These characters struggle to separate justified rage from revenge, victims from villains. Richard Marsh's Judith Lee fiercely wishes harm upon her assaulters but insists that it is not "revenge only." We catch a glimpse of the genre's opportunities for clarity around right and wrong in early works such as Pauline E. Hopkins's *Hagar's Daughter* (2021a). But we also see the simultaneous complications, where violence is excessive or justice elusive. The challenges of making injustice visible is shown by the trope of racial passing in two of the first female detective stories by Hopkins.

"Using It" looks at some paradigmatic examples of the dominant form of female-centered crime narrative of the past fifty years: the strong female sleuth. In so doing, I skip over the fifty years between Judith Lee's fin-de-siecle fury and V. I. Warshawski's second-wave rage. Part of this leap is due to the brevity of this Element. But I have chosen this moment in the timeline to omit because critics have seen this as an unusual time for female detectives. Tatar writes that "oddly, there is something of a midlife crisis in the universe of woman detectives in the first half of the twentieth century, for it is dominated either by girls investigating or by spinsters sleuthing" (Tatar 2021: 154). Others see the questions about anger and identity manifesting in works less explicitly

---

[27] The controversy surrounding the now-closed Staunch book prize, founded by Bridget Lawless and awarded to a work in the genre in which no woman is "beaten, stalked, sexually exploited, raped or murdered" (http://staunchbookprize.com/about-2/), reveals the challenges in representing violence against women. Crime writers, including Val McDermid and Julia Couch, pushed back against such restrictions, noting that violence against women was a reality and they were obligated to represent it (www.theguardian.com/books/2019/jul/05/crime-writers-react-staunch-prize-claim-hinder-rape-trials).

interested in detection and justice, and more interested in criminality and psychology. Novels by Patricia Highsmith, Vera Caspary, Helen Eustis, Dorothy B. Hughes, Evelyn Piper, and Elisabeth Sanxay Holding contain messy female feelings. Golden Age works of Sayers and Christie have complicated affects, though there, too, we see efforts to "use it." There are almost certainly lots of noncanonical texts drawing a clearer connection between works such as *Hagar's Daughter* and *Blanche on the Lam* that are beyond the scope of this work.[28] This is not a survey; there are lots of missing persons. But partly I leap from the turn of the century to the 1980s because the explicit conversation second-wave feminism wanted to have about anger, represented by Lorde's "The Use of Anger," was an origin point for me as well as for other scholars of the genre.

"Using It" focuses on second-wave feminism's understanding of anger as a political force and how that shapes the rise of the individualist female detective hero in series fiction of the 1980–2000s, such as in Sara Paretsky's V. I. Warshawski novels. Writers working in that vein today, such as Denise Mina in her Alex Morrow series, are modifying aspects of that story. Female writers of color over the course of this time both use and challenge individualism in their own fights for justice. Barbara Neely's Blanche White (1992–2000) is a crucial figure for exploring how intersectional feminism finds a home in female-centered crime narratives, as she navigates both structural violence and stereotypes around the Angry Black Woman. Writers of color working more recently, such as Steph Cha, Cheryl A. Head, and Lauren Wilkinson, build on Neely's legacy. All of the writers in this section explore care and community as important elements of or alternatives to justice. But they are also complexly embedded in structures of seething. We see in these works that anger needs to be clear to be productive; but we also see our sleuths struggle with this demand, both in their personal relationships and in the muted closure that many books provide.

"Losing It" observes a more recent turn in crime narratives to violence and despair, responding to perceptions of today's stalled social change. Bogutskaya writes that the "2010s did not invent unlikeable, unruly women. There were *plenty* before. But we did, finally, develop the language to understand and articulate what social tensions these characters were tapping into" (Bogutskaya 2023: 27). In these texts, narratives of justice are engaged but largely abandoned. This section looks at the "pessimistic critique" represented

---

[28] Works such as Clarke 2020 and Hefner 2021 suggest that what we currently know of crime fiction of the nineteenth and early twentieth century, which often ran in ephemeral publications (local and regional newspapers), might only be the tip of the iceberg. Indeed, Emily Cline (2022) has drawn recent attention to Catherine Crowe's *Adventures of Susan Hopley: or, Circumstantial Evidence* (1841).

by domestic noir (Redhead 2018: 131) in writers such as Gillian Flynn, Paula Hawkins, and Megan Abbott, and considers the rise of the assassin in Natsuo Kirino's *Out*, Gu Byeong-Mo's *The Old Woman with the Knife*, and *Killing Eve*. The affective states of these violent texts are complicated; they pitch from humor and camp to horror and gore. Such ultraviolent stories may satisfy feminist expressions of anger, but not necessarily feminist aims of, as Lorde writes, "progress and change." This Element concludes with an Epilogue that offers no solutions, but reads Michaela Coel's *I May Destroy You* (2020) as a paradigmatic example of the affordances of structures of seething, the destructive and redemptive waiting where questions of justice live now.

2 Mad?

While women would not officially serve in police departments in the US and the UK until the early twentieth century, they have been patrolling the pages of detective fiction as imaginary characters since the mid-nineteenth century. These accidental, amateur, and police-adjacent sleuths are searching both for answers to particular mysteries (deaths, disappearances, secret identities, contested wills) and to broader injustices in worlds where they have few civil rights. Wilkie Collins's Anne Rodway, a poor needlewoman, channels her anger at the violent death of her boardinghouse roommate into one of the first female detective stories, "The Diary of Anne Rodway" (1856). Women in the Sherlock Holmes stories provide tantalizing glimpses of the potential for anger to lead to justice, but most visitors to Baker Street are socially vulnerable and seeking male assistance; some simply want revenge. Through the first decades of the twentieth century, female sleuths like Richard Marsh's Judith Lee and Anna Katharine Green's Violet Strange are sometimes rageful or sometimes have a more suspended affect, but their tales reveal the precarity of female life in remarkably violent worlds. Venus Johnson's brief, dazzling appearance in Hopkins's *Hagar's Daughter* illustrates how this figure might marshal her anger in the fight for justice.

Women are motivated by anger in these early crime narratives; however, their agency is curtailed or complicated, forecasting a problematic future for the angry female detective. Collins's female detective figures, such as Marian in *The Woman in White* and Valeria Woodcourt in *The Law and the Lady*, get almost all the way to a solution and then are sidelined by domestic arrangements. All the detective figures considered in this section are only partially effective in stories where justice remains unfinished business. One of the things that compromises the search for justice is the muddling of anger and madness. Female madness in nineteenth-century literature has long been seen as a metaphor for expressing rage and rebellion. Catherine Ross Nickerson's *The Web of Iniquity: Early Detective*

Fiction by American Women explores the "conventions that constitute a language for expressing female anger and rebellion" in nineteenth-century detective fiction (Nickerson 1998: xi). Sandra Gilbert and Susan Gubar's classic *Madwoman in the Attic* is about both female rage and the blurry line between anger and madness. In keeping with our angry times, they have recently followed up with *Still Mad*, which is more focused on anger, "the rebellious rage of the madwoman we studied, a female figure incensed by patriarchal structures that have proven to be shockingly obdurate" (Gilbert & Gubar 2021: 7). We are still sorting out the relationship between anger, madness, and feminist reimaginations of a more just society.

2.1 Half-Angry: Lady Audley and Anne Rodway

As anyone who has been called a "crazy bitch" knows, invoking madness is an efficient way to dismiss women's anger. While this has probably been going on since the first caveman was asked to take out the trash, it is a particularly well-documented phenomenon in women's writings about their experiences in asylums in the nineteenth century. A collection edited by Jeffrey L. Geller and Maxine Harris, with an Introduction by psychologist Phyllis Chesler (author of the 1972 feminist classic *Women and Madness*), includes writings from women institutionalized between 1840 and 1945 (including Charlotte Perkins Gilman). These writers document a catch-22: women who, out of anger, resist rules are locked up and then, once locked up, can go mad. Elizabeth Parsons Ware Packard, an advocate for wrongfully confined women, succinctly expresses it in her "Bill No. 1": "No person shall be regarded or treated as an Insane person, or a Monomaniac, simply for the expression of opinions, no matter how absurd these opinions may appear to others" (Geller & Harris 1994: 66). Monomania, according to Packard, "in many instances is not Insanity, but individuality" (Geller & Harris 1994: 68). Phebe B. Davis makes the same point about her time in the New York Lunatic Asylum at Utica: the "great trouble in Lunatic Asylums" is that they "have their written rules, and all who cannot be cured by being subjected to their code of laws are pronounced incurable at once; and their rules are enough to make a rational person crazy" (Geller & Harris, 1994: 57).

The fiction of this time famously reflects and, at times, revels in this problem. Sensation fiction arose in the 1860s, combining Gothic and domestic realist modes both for entertainment and to grapple with very real injustices facing women. Elaine Showalter's *A Literature of Their Own* covers the novels of this period; in it, she argues that the novels' "secrets were not simply solutions to mysteries and crimes; they were the secrets of women's dislike of their roles as daughters, wives, and mothers ... Readers were introduced to a new kind of heroine, one who could put her hostility toward men into violent action" (Showalter 1977: 158–160). No novel from this period better expresses the bladerunning between anger and madness than Mary Elizabeth Braddon's *Lady Audley's Secret* (1987 [1862]). The novel tells the story of a beautiful but poor newlywed, Lucy Talboys, whose husband, George, is disowned by his rich father and then abandons her and their infant son to seek his fortune in Australia. Lucy reinvents herself in one of the few ways available to women at the time by becoming a governess, beginning a pattern of hiding secrets that will ultimately overwhelm her, signified by a ring on a black ribbon she nervously clutches around her neck. A rich older neighbor, Sir Michael Audley, is bewitched by Lucy's youthful charms and proposes. When George's return three years later threatens to expose Lucy's bigamy, she pushes him down a well. Lucy plays a cat-and-mouse game with Sir Michael's nephew, Robert, who wonders what happened to his old friend, George.

While Lady Audley is described as a child-like beauty, the "fragile blond angel of domestic realism" (Showalter 1977: 165), Braddon tells us from the very beginning that she is complicated. When Lucy learns that Sir Michael means to propose to her, she turns ghostly pale and starts "fidget[ing] nervously with the ribbon, clutching at it with a half-angry gesture." Lucy says that "some people are born to be unlucky" and that "it would be a great too much good fortune for me to become Lady Audley" (Braddon 1987: 9). Braddon notes that Lucy "said this with so much bitterness in her tone, that the surgeon's wife looked up at her with surprise" (Braddon 1987: 9). The reader wonders what Lucy is "half-angry" about, and Braddon suggests this reads as a kind of madness by her employers, who "would have thought it something more than madness in a penniless girl to reject such an offer" (Braddon 1987: 9). Sir Michael thinks this, too, so he is surprised when he asks her to marry him out of love and gets a mini-lecture on structural violence. Lucy rants:

> remember what my life has been ... from my very babyhood I have never seen anything but poverty. My father was a gentleman; clever, accomplished, generous, handsome – but poor. My mother – But do not let me speak of her. Poverty, poverty, trials, vexations, humiliations, deprivations! *You* cannot tell; you, who are amongst those for whom life is so smooth and easy; you can never guess what is endured by such as we ... I *cannot* be disinterested.
> (Braddon 1987: 10–11)

Lucy's feelings are described as a "passionate vehemence" (Braddon 1987: 11); there is "an undefined something in her manner which filled the baronet with a vague alarm" (Braddon 1987: 11). Sir Michael slips into the language of economics when he agrees to a "bargain" but feels like he "carried a corpse in his bosom" (Braddon 1987:11). Lucy's feelings are strong, but unclear, grounded in both structural violence and personal ambition. She is "half-angry" and "something more than mad."

That the feelings raging in this blond, doll-like governess are dangerous is the animating spirit of the novel. And we know what happens to dangerous women in the nineteenth century. "Buried alive" is the name of the chapter near the end of *Lady Audley's Secret* where Robert, having unearthed the mystery of her past, takes Lady Audley to an asylum in Europe. She lays her hand on Robert's arm and says "I know where you have brought me. This is a MAD-HOUSE" (Braddon 1987: 387). Feisty to the end, she balks at his attempts to rebrand it a *maison de santé*. Showalter argues that "Lady Audley's real secret is that she is *sane* and, moreover, representative" (Braddon 1987: 167). The novel mostly agrees. In some of the most validating sentences contained in a Victorian novel, one of the doctors who examines Lady Audley says

> there is no evidence of madness in anything that she has done. She ran away from her home, because her home was not a pleasant one, and she left it in the hope of finding a better. There is no madness in that. She committed the crime of bigamy, because by that crime she obtained fortune and position. There is no madness there. When she found herself in a desperate position, she did not grow desperate. She employed intelligent means, and she carried out a conspiracy which required coolness and deliberation in its execution. There is no madness in that. (Braddon 1987: 377)

The doctor allows that she may have a hint of "latent insanity," which descends from her mother, but the novel allows Lady Audley to speak about that for herself: "He did not know the hidden taint that I had sucked in with my mother's milk. He did not know that it was possible to drive me mad" (Braddon 1987: 393).

Braddon doesn't really try to clean this up. After telling the reader that Lady Audley dies in the asylum, she provides a classically happy ending while implying that she is both anticipating and overruling readerly objections: "I hope no one will take objection to my story because the end of it leaves the good people all happy and at peace" (Braddon 1987: 447). If the readers have taken objection, it is because, while narrative demands are fulfilled, justice may not be. Part of what is going on here is the friction between two genres. *Lady Audley Secret* is one of the defining works of sensation fiction (along with Collins's 1860 *The Woman in White* and Ellen Wood's 1861 *East Lynne*); as such, it lets out the emotional throttle. It's a yawp, whose descendants are those emotionally messy novels of domestic noir. But *Lady Audley's Secret* is also famous for being an early example of detective fiction, a genre arguably more geared toward regulation and justice. Much has been written about how Robert Audley goes from a barely employed, French-novel-reading layabout to a practicing lawyer cum family man on a fine estate because he is called to detection. We see him shaking off the sloth, finding charred remains of documents in the fire, checking train tables, interviewing witnesses. Anger is clarifying for Robert as he seeks justice for men: his potentially murdered friend George, and his uncle, tricked into a bigamous marriage. This enables him to become a new man, or, to borrow Lauren Berlant's phrase, "the logic of responsible affective self-management" is at the core of both his bourgeois transformation and his pursuit of justice. It is harder for women to focus their anger and perform this transformation (they have their hands on fewer ropes than Robert Audley), as we see with some of our first fictional female sleuths.

"The Diary of Anne Rodway," by Wilkie Collins, opened the July 19, 1856 installment of Charles Dickens's weekly journal *Household Words*, and concluded the following week. Arguably one of the earliest appearances of a female sleuth in literature (as far as we know), it tells the story of the mysterious death of Mary Mallinson, a needlewoman and boardinghouse companion of Anne Rodway, also a needlewoman as well as the narrator and eventual sleuth. It also explicitly links justice with anger in Anne's critique of power. Anne's solidarity with Mary, her anger at their mistreatment as working-class women, and their broader vulnerability in a patriarchal economy drive her investigation. Sometimes this bends toward justice; sometimes toward revenge. Ultimately, in what is a trend in nineteenth-century female-centered crime fiction, Anne will be sidelined by a male character who wraps up the investigation in her stead.

Collins makes clear from the first lines that this story is about the abuse of power, and puts these words in Anne's mouth. Anne writes in her diary that the

> clergyman said in his sermon last Sunday evening that all things were ordered for the best, and we are all put into the stations in life that are properest for us. I suppose he was right, being a very clever gentleman who fills the church to crowding; but I think I should have understood him better if I had not been very hungry at the time in consequence of my own station in life being nothing but a poor needlewoman. (Collins 1856: 1)

The clergyman is joined in this story by others who abuse their authority: Anne's landlord, the "inhuman wretch who owns the house and lives in idleness on the high rents he wrings from poor people like us" (Collins 1856: 4) and who ultimately threatens Anne with having Mary's corpse seized to get her to pay Mary's back rent; Mary's employers, who contribute to her death by sending her home faint with hunger late at night and alone, and are reproved at the inquest; and the Church, faulted for requiring so many small charges for "burying poor people" (Collins 1856: 6),

The story also makes clear that poverty shapes people's emotional lives. Anne's fiancé, Robert, is in America trying to make enough money for them to marry. As in Braddon, this is no fairy tale: though Anne "loves him dearly," she "cannot look forward to meeting him again, disappointed and broken down, and poorer than ever" (Collins 1856: 330–1). When she thinks of their reunion, it is with a "feeling of almost dread." She doesn't dread this for herself so much, as women "are more patient than men." But she dreads "Robert's despondency," and the emotional labor required to sustain a relationship in financial straits. So, an early female-centered crime story takes pains to locate the character in violent structural forces and to reveal her navigation of her feelings. We have access to these feelings because the story is told by Anne via her diary, which makes the personal political quite directly and underscores the connection between her feelings for Mary and her motivations in solving the case. Anne considers Mary "the sister of my love," taking her under her wing when she fled an abusive step-mother. (This evil step-mother, however, is not a two-dimensional fairy tale villain. Mary's "abuse and ill usage" is linked to the abuse the step-mother suffered from Mary's alcoholic father. Patriarchy hurts everyone.) Anne's feelings are hard to put into words: "I feel as if I could go to the world's end to serve that girl. Yet, strange to say, if I was asked why I was so fond of her, I don't think I should know how to answer that question" (Collins 1856: 3). Anne has strong feelings, but they aren't entirely clear.

Anne's interest in Mary, however, becomes clearer the next evening when Mary doesn't return home. An oafish policeman shows up with Mary's body; she has suffered an unexplained blow to the head. Anne is transformed, represented by an unprecedented break in the journal: "for three days I have not been able to write a single line in this journal, which I have kept so regularly, ever since I was a girl" (Collins 1856: 3). Anne is furious at the policeman's dismissal of Mary and his questioning of her sobriety: "I could have struck the man for uttering the word" (Collins 1856: 4). Anne is having a good cry over Mary's expiring body when she finds a clue: a piece of a torn cravat in Mary's hand. Anne is joined by "Dusty Sal," the maid of all work, who takes a turn watching Mary's body, underscoring the working-class female solidarity that provides care where there is no justice. Anne feels a "fever of anxiety" that Mary will die before shedding light on this clue, but the search anchors her: "the straits and difficulties I am in keep my mind on the stretch" (Collins 1856: 6).

Justice for Mary requires Anne to regulate her feelings. In the face of her "brutal and pitiless landlord" demanding Mary's backrent, she is "determined not to let him see how he had horrified me, if I could possibly control myself ... [because] there was no good and no help in tears" (Collins 1856: 30). As frequently happens in Collins's fiction, Anne has a dream. In it, she is urged by an angel with Mary's voice and eyes to pursue the truth, which "is waiting for you to find it" (Collins 1856: 32). The next diary entry begins "I have found it!" (meaning the rest of the cravat from which the fragment in Mary's hand was torn) and the game is afoot. Anne still toggles between the discipline of writing in her diary and the overwhelming "nervousness and uncertainty" which prevents it (Collins 1856: 33). The uncertainty underscores that Anne has no framework for understanding herself as an agent of justice; instead, she writes that "a kind of fever got possession of me – a vehement yearning to go on from this first discovery and find out more, no matter what the risk might be" (Collins 1856: 33). When her search leads her to the original wearer of the torn cravat, Anne describes her detective fever as an out-of-body experience:

> My head got giddy and my eyes seemed able to see nothing but the figure of the little crooked-backed man ... The minute before, there had been no idea of me speaking to him ... something out of myself seemed to ... make me speak without considering beforehand, without thinking of consequences, without knowing, I may almost say, what words I was uttering till the instant when they rose to my lips. (Collins 1856: 33–34)

Like a natural detective, Anne cleverly keeps the man, a cab driver, talking and learns the heart of the mystery: Mary was knocked to her death by a man catching the cab.

She is reeling from her discovery when she returns home to find Robert, back from America. She rushes into the room "like a mad woman" (Collins 1856: 35). Collins doesn't intend for us to understand Anne as a shrewd sleuth in one minute and losing her senses in the next. But it is also true that this is the beginning of the end of her detective work, for what are described as mental health reasons. Robert picks up the case: "it was best that he would carry out the rest of the investigation alone, for my strength and resolution had been too hardly taxed already" (Collins 1856: 35). Anne is sidelined: "I am writing these lines alone while he has gone to the Mews to treat with the dastardly, heartless wretch with whom I spoke yesterday" (Collins 1856: 35).[29]

Anne experiences a range of responses to the outcome. At first she seems oriented to revenge: "I shall know no ease of mind until her murderer is secured, and till I am certain that he will be made to suffer for his crimes" (Collins 1856: 36).

---

[29] This will happen time and again in nineteenth century stories, especially in Collins, who creates fascinating female sleuths only to hobble them at the end. Marian in *The Woman in White*, Valeria Woodville in *The Law and the Lady*, and Magdalen Vanstone in *No Name* are important early female detective figures from whom the final solution of the mystery is denied. As Michelle Slung writes, female sleuths are finished off "not at the Reichenbach Falls, but at the matrimonial altar" (Slung 1975: xx).

When Anne learns that the charge will be manslaughter, she writes that she "accepted the explanation but it did not satisfy me. Mary Mallinson was killed by the blow from the hand of Noah Truscott. That is murder in the sight of God. Why not murder in the sight of the law also?" (Collins 1856: 36). Ultimately, however, she sees the limitations of vengeance: "The law does indeed punish Noah Truscott for his crime, but can it raise up Mary Mallinson from her last resting-place in the churchyard?" (Collins 1856: 37). The mood at the end of the story is mixed. Nothing will bring back Mary, whose death has exposed the reader to the everyday crimes of patriarchal violence that render the women in the story vulnerable, their murders easily dismissed as "accidental." Angry women and abusive men abound in this story. Even the discovery of the cravat-wearer is framed by two stories of domestic violence: Anne encounters a woman being abused by a man in the shop, who then "rather angrily" tells her a story of another woman who dropped the rags there, "a poor creature with a lazy brute of a husband" (Collins 1856: 32). This woman is angry too: when Anne finds her and asks about taking the cravat to sell at the shop, she says "bitterly" that she wishes she could have "pitched [her husband] in after it. I'd sell him cheap at any ragshop" (Collins 1856: 33). Though Anne is sidelined in the investigation, she does offer testimony in court, playing a part in securing justice.

2.2 Turn of the Century Tales

Women's peripheral role in the operations of official justice are the subject of two novels that appeared in 1864: William Stephens Hayward's *Revelations of a Lady Detective* and Andrew Forrester's *The Female Detective*. These collections of episodes featuring female sleuths notably brought women into a conversation about justice, but did not inaugurate a rash of novels featuring female sleuths. The critical connective tissue between mid-century female detectives and turn-of-the century "sisters of Sherlock" is still being built.[30] But we are all familiar with Baker Street, and vulnerable women are frequent visitors there. Lisa Surridge remarks that "a striking number of Sherlock Holmes stories deal with abuse of women, ranging from coercion and imprisonment to assault and murder," and that they mostly participate in a reassuring narrative about the need for male protection (Surridge 2005: 226–228). Nevertheless, in the Holmes stories we see a range of responses to this abuse, from using it to losing it. In "The Adventure of the Copper Beeches," Violet Hunter illustrates serious detective instincts as she

---

[30] See Nickerson (1998) and Clarke (2020), as well as the stories collected in *The Penguin Book of Victorian Women in Crime*, ed. Michael Sims (Penguin, 2011), and *Early American Detective Stories: An Anthology*, ed. LeRoy Lad Panek and Mary M. Bendel-Simso (McFarland & Company, Inc. 2008). As noted earlier, I suspect what we know might only be a tip of the periodical press iceberg.

works to protect herself and solve the mystery of her threatening new employers. She tells Holmes and Watson that,

> from the moment that I understood that there was something about that suite of rooms which I was not to know, I was all on fire to go over them. It was not mere curiosity, though I have my share of that. It was more a feeling of duty – a feeling that some good might come from my penetrating to this place. They talk of woman's instinct; perhaps it was woman's instinct which gave me that feeling. (Conan Doyle 1977: 281)

In "Charles Augustus Milverton," Holmes and Watson break into the home of Milverton, a notorious blackmailer, in order to steal his evidence. When the blackmailed victim, "the woman whose life you have ruined," confronts Milverton, he says he "will make allowance for [her] natural anger" (Conan Doyle 1994: 164, 171) and invites her to leave. She does not, and instead drew "a little gleaming revolver, and emptied barrel after barrel into Milverton's body." On her way out, she "ground her heel into his upturned face" (Conan Doyle 1994: 172). This display of both revenge murder and gratuitous violence is approved of by Holmes: "there are certain crimes which the law cannot touch, and which therefore, to some extent, justify private revenge" (Conan Doyle 1994: 174). While women are mostly vulnerable and seeking help (Violet Hunter seeks them out because "I have no parents or relations of any sort from whom I could ask advice"; "The Adventures of the Copper Beeches," Conan Doyle 1977: 265), in detective fiction's most formative series, there is not a clear message about the relationship between female anger and justice. Structures of seething allow us to see women as vulnerable and sidelined, but also curious and agentic, sorting through a variety of angry responses from taking revenge to stepping aside to seeking justice.

One of the angriest female detectives in literary history joined Holmes on the pages of *The Strand*. Richard Marsh's "The Man Who Cut Off My Hair" introduces us to Judith Lee, who is transformed into a sleuth at age twelve by virtue of a violent assault. Lee is the hero of twenty-two stories that ran in *The Strand* between 1911 and 1916. It had become a crowded detective fiction field, as *The Strand* recognized in its introduction to the series: "a new detective method is such a rare thing that it is with unusual pleasure we introduce our readers to Judith Lee, the fortunate possessor of a gift which gives her a place in detective fiction." The gift is a seemingly minor one: she can read lips, and, while on a train, reads the lips of two strangers hatching a plot to rob her neighbor. When she goes to her neighbor's home and is noticed watching, she is bound, gagged, and threatened with murder with lines like "if you try to scream I'll twist your head right off you" and "slit her throat and get done with it" (Marsh 2016: 5). But what incites Judith's rage is that they cut her long, beautiful hair – according to her mother, "the glory of a woman" – and then proceed to strike her across the face with it. Judith writes "If I could have got within reach of him at that moment I believe that I should have stuck that knife into him. Rage made me half beside myself" (Marsh 2016: 6). She is clear that she feels anger, not fear: "I was not afraid; I can honestly say that I have seldom been afraid of anything" (Marsh, 2016: 8). She understands that her anger might look like madness: "I believe that for a moment they thought that what I had endured had turned my brain, and that I was mad. But I soon made it perfectly clear that I was nothing of the kind" (Marsh 2016: 10). The rage is not maddening, it is productive. She looks in a looking-glass and "when I saw what I looked like the rage which had possessed me when the outrage first took place surged through me with greater force than ever" (Marsh 2016: 9). She joins a team of police in pursuit of the criminals, eager to "be even with the man." She knows how this sounds: "I daresay it sounds as if I were very revengeful. I do not think it was a question of vengeance only; I wanted justice" (Marsh 2016: 14–15). But, as the "only" suggests, it is mixed. The series contains a range of complicated emotions, and resolutions over the course of the stories are more unsettling than just.

American author Anna Katharine Green, who corresponded with Conan Doyle, and who Agatha Christie credits with inspiring her, had two female sleuths. Green's spinster sleuth was Amelia Butterworth. She is a straightforward, sensible semi-meddler, who realizes that "it would never do for me to lose my wits in the presence of a man who had none too many of his" (Green 2013: 3). Green's Violet Strange, a young woman who appears in a series of stories collected as *The Golden Slipper* (1915), is far harder to read. Neither of these female characters is extraordinarily "likable," in the way of Grant Allen's Hilda Wade or Lois Cayley. Violet, a debutante who assists a private detective on cases for special clients, is irritable and unsentimental. The cases reveal a world full of violence against women (*That Affair Next Door*, a Butterworth mystery, also begins with a female corpse). "An Intangible Clue" follows the murder of a woman in the home where she was born, married, and lived until her death, the arc of her life shrunk down to its patriarchal basics. Violet, hearing of the shocking murder, says coldly, "I am interested in the house, not her" (Green 1997: 148) and "you're trying to interest me in the woman. Don't" (Green 1997: 149). But Green interests the reader, painting a vivid picture of the crime: "She fought – her dress was torn from her body in rags ... and she was dragged from room to room" (Green 1997: 148). While Violet solves the crime, there is no broader commentary about justice for this violated woman.

In *Hagar's Daughter*, one of the earliest African American crime novels and the first (as far as we know) to feature a Black female sleuth, and an earlier short story, "Talma Gordon," Pauline E. Hopkins turns the genre toward social justice, illustrating how anger – on the part of both author and characters – could be harnessed in the fight. In both works, Hopkins employs the metaphor of racial passing for the fraudulence of American justice. Passing, a structure of seething, signals a potentially disruptive energy troubling the surface of society.[31] "Talma Gordon" is about the violent killing of a family, including a father of a disinherited daughter. The eponymous daughter is acquitted but suspicion lingers. A deathbed confession clears her name, and reveals Talma's mixed race ancestry. It also reveals the character of nineteenth-century white society: her fiancé leaves her, saying "I could stand the stigma of murder, but add to that the pollution of Negro blood! No man is brave enough to face such a situation" (Hopkins, 2021b: 317). The "crime" of passing returns in much greater detail in *Hagar's Daughter*, the subtitle of which reveals its centrality: "A Story of Southern Caste Prejudice." The novel's events take place at two different time periods: the first half begins in the fall of 1860, when the nomination of Abraham Lincoln ensures the outbreak of civil war; the second half twenty years later, during Reconstruction. This gap in time aids the crime narrative plot: it enables the disappearance and reappearance of vaguely familiar characters (named Enson, Benson, and Henson), the contesting of inheritances, and the settling of old scores. The gap in the narrative also serves as a report card on American democracy: how're we doing twenty years after Appomattox? The answer: barely passing.

When the novel begins, two sons of an aristocratic Maryland family, Ellis and St. Clair Enson, gather at the family estate. Ellis is the rightful heir and new husband to Hagar and father to a baby daughter; St. Clair is the scheming younger brother, who is first glimpsed plotting secession at the convention in Charleston, South Carolina, and whom the narrative later implies was in on the Lincoln assassination. On his way back to Maryland, St. Clair falls in with a "notorious slave-trader," who provides the information that his brother's beautiful wife is a formerly enslaved person, an "octoroon" that he himself had sold to a childless couple years ago. As in "Talma Gordon," the crime of concealed "Negro blood" – of passing as white – trumps all the other crimes happening around them, from treason and murder to blackmail and slavery. Ellis feels disgraced at the revelation. He decides to leave Hagar but ultimately comes up with a plan for them to live together abroad: the problem is not his young family, but the country in which they live. Before he can make arrangements, however, a dead body believed to be his is discovered on the estate.

---

[31] Chen (2005: 16), discussing Pamela Caughie's *Passing and Pedagogy: The Dynamics of Responsibility* (University of Illinois Press, 1999), suggests that passing represents the "ghostly ... markers of identity," a "performance in multiple registers" that haunts American society and keeps semivisible its racial history and politics.

Hagar and her child are taken by the slave-trader to be sold into slavery and, in case we miss the point, not just anywhere but in a slave market in the nation's capital, Washington, DC. Hagar avoids this fate when, holding her baby, she jumps into the Potomac River. The river carries them out of our view until, twenty years later, a character who would be just the age of that baby if she'd managed to survive a plunge into the Potomac appears on the scene as Jewel, the beloved adopted daughter of a US senator.

Female anger in nineteenth-century crime fiction is mostly indirect; this makes sense when anger could get you thrown into an asylum by your own family. Where men rage in *Hagar's Daughter*, the women harbor "vague feeling[s] of distrust and dislike" (Hopkins 2021a: 125) and "a loathing" they "could not repress." "[H]ot anger" briefly flashes, but returns to quiet seething. The female emotion in this novel is more visible in its Gothic conventions. As Catherine Ross Nickerson has pointed out, Gothic conventions in early American crime fiction "constitute a language for expressing female anger and rebellion" (Nickerson 1998: xi). *Hagar's Daughter* contains an "ancient ruin," where the kidnapped Jewel is held in order to preserve a wrongful inheritance:

> The main body of the stately dwelling was standing, but scarcely a vestige of the once beautiful outbuildings remained: the cabins in the slave quarters stood like skeletons beneath the nodding leaves and beckoning arms of the grand old beeches. War and desolation had done their best to reduce the stately pile to a wreck. It bore, too, an uncanny reputation. The Negroes declared that the beautiful woods and the lonely avenues were haunted after nightfall. (Hopkins 2021a: 222)

Jewel does not meet a ghost, but rather a kindly old woman, Aunt Henny, who has also been abducted to prevent her testimony in the murder trial of Jewel's fiancé, Cuthbert Sumner. Both Jewel and Henny will be rescued by the first Black female sleuth (that we know of), Venus Johnson, who is also the old woman's granddaughter and Jewel's servant. Venus cross-dresses as a boy, giving her more mobility to track down the missing women and enter the home. Venus's sleuthing is driven by anger at male mistreatment of women (Hopkins 2021a: 215), including that of her own father, and the injustice faced by Jewel. "The police are slower 'n death," she thinks, and "Dad's up to his capers. He can fool ma, but he can't pull the wool over my eyes; I'm his daughter. Hump! ... It's a burning shame for dad to go on this way after all Miss Jewel's kindness to us. But I'll balk him. I'll see him out on this case or my name ain't Venus Johnson" (Hopkins 2021a: 217). She resolves to herself "I'll see if this one little black girl can't get the best of as mean a set of villains as ever was born" (Hopkins 2021a: 217). Her discovery enables Henny to testify in Sumner's murder trial. In the trial scene, to which Hopkins dedicates several chapters, American jurisprudence is shown poised between justice and mob rule. The US Attorney-General hypocritically denounces "violence of any kind as beneath the dignity of our calling," yet says that if justice were not done, he "would feel myself justified in sounding the slogan of the South – lynch law" (Hopkins 2021a: 245).

Hopkins doesn't have mob rule carry the day. Sumner is exonerated based on both Aunt Henny's testimony and the dramatic courtroom disclosure that Senator Benson's widow is Hagar. However, racial passing complicates the operations of justice. Sumner's "trial" isn't over. Jewel's ancestry as Hagar's daughter is ultimately revealed, and Sumner can't see past his caste prejudice. He waits longer than Ellis did to have a change of heart. When he does, it is too late; on the final page, he (and the reader) are left discovering Jewel's untimely grave, and questioning "wherein he had sinned and why he was so severely punished" (Hopkins 2021a: 266). Hopkins provides an immediate answer: "the sin is the nation's" (Hopkins 2021a: 266). This first African American crime novel (that we know of) written by a Black woman contains several different stories, but they all circle back to the "crime" of passing as a metaphor for the unfinished business of American justice. The novel's double time frame spotlights that the US has always been guilty of passing as a democracy, from its origins in genocide and slavery to the extralegal threat of lynching that limns the American courtroom. Having the relatively triumphant courtroom scene, where Black women's words mattered, take place prior to Sumner's prejudice and punishment, as Nickerson writes, "deliberately thwarts emotional closure" (Nickerson 1998: 55). It keeps us waiting. Martin notes that sometimes "waiting is no longer waiting to know something. Rather, it is waiting to see how the detective's knowledge will turn out to make a difference – or not to – in the world at large" (Martin 2019: 103). The sleuths we follow in the next section will try to use their knowledge, and their anger, to make a difference.

3 Using It

Most crime narratives written at any period of time contain some character marshaling their feelings to bring about a just resolution. "Using it" is still the predominant practice in female-centered crime narrative, with many of the writers discussed here continuing to publish new novels on a regular basis, and many television sleuths organized around the principle of using anger to fight for justice (I see you, Olivia Benson). But this section takes as its start the female detective fiction emerging in the wake of the Civil Rights movement of the 1960s and 1970s, which gave the fight against injustice a new vocabulary, and women writers and characters a more frank conversation about anger and its affordances. These narratives celebrate both feminist agency and anger in a wide variety of individual sleuths, as well as highlight some of the tensions around individualism and systemic change that shape this moment of feminist history and its legacies into the twenty-first century. The enormous variety of fiction and sleuths who use their anger is well beyond the scope of the Element.[32] The authors chosen here represent some of the major tensions in the expression of female anger and its connections to justice; intersectional issues, structural violence, and partial victories thicken the structures of seething. The section begins by looking at Sara Paretsky's private detective V. I. Warshawski and Denise Mina's Glaswegian Detective Chief Inspector Alex Morrow as two examples of tough, complicated justice warriors, fighting through traumatic backgrounds. Anger is never too far from the surface in these texts. Paretsky paved the way for the kind of anger Morrow experiences, and Mina attempts to challenge some of the limitations of second-wave feminist imaginings.

Whether in the twentieth or early twenty-first centuries, both Warshawski and Morrow, being white, have the privilege to be publicly angry in ways that are more complicated for women of color. This section also examines sleuths of color, such as Barbara Neely's Blanche White, Steph Cha's Juniper Song, Cheryl Head's Charlie Mack, and Lauren Wilkinson's Marie Mitchell. These characters use anger to seek justice, but also to interrogate the priorities and outcomes of second-wave feminism. It is worth remembering that Lorde's "Uses of Anger" had almost as much to do with anger between women around race and sexuality as it did about anger toward the patriarchy. The idea of passing reappears here, signaling, as it did in Hopkins, unfinished business around racial justice that troubles the surface of society. Vexed relations around sisterhood reflect the genre's commitment to individualism as well as the work still to be done in building solidarity. Blanche is a ferocious reporter from the frontlines of the intersections between racism, sexism, ableism, and classism, and, over the course of the series, teeters between ancestor-worshipping community healer and self-destructive loner. Song is in a continual self-imposed compare-and-contrast with Chandler's Philip Marlowe, showing how and why hard-boiled anger presents particular challenges for a young Korean-American

---

[32] As discussed in the Introduction, this Element skips most of the first half of the twentieth century, which is full of angry, complicated women, represented by pulp and noir writing in the US and portraits of both regulation and ugly feelings in British Golden Age detective narratives. This period also saw major shifts in how we understand the self, as well as the development and fragility of the mind. See Walton 2015.

female sleuth. Head's Charlie Mack is a member of a mixed gender, multiracial investigation team, challenging our ideas about the individualism celebrated by the genre. Lauren Wilkinson, nudging the genre toward spy fiction and not (as far as we know) creating a series sleuth in the character of Marie, shows us a character who carefully controls her anger, but who finds sisterhood a mystery and justice indistinguishable from revenge.

Around the time Lorde asked women to use their anger, three influential series sleuths emerged: two out of California – Marcia Muller's Sharon McCone and Sue Grafton's Kinsey Millhone – and Paretsky's Warshawski. The fact that the genre found momentum with the figure of the private detective, rather than the cop on the force, suggests that skepticism about official justice is baked into female-centered crime narrative. As is white privilege. Admittedly, Sharon McCone has some Shoshone ancestry and part of the sleuth's multi-decade journey has been understanding how this shapes her identity in real time (the first novel appeared in 1977, the 35th is out this year). But Millhone and Paretsky are both white. Millhone shares a lot with the sleuths in this section: a history of trauma (as a child, she lost her parents in a gruesome car accident), insubordination (why she left the police department), wry feminist insights ("the basic characteristics of any good investigator are a plodding nature and infinite patience. Society has inadvertently been grooming women to this end for years"),[33] and an interrogation of justice (the first novel alone features a miscarriage of justice, revenge killings, and some decent cops). But Millhone is committed to containment. In the wake of killing a lover, she doesn't like being part of the nastiness, but she admits "I'll recover, of course. I'll be ready for business again in a week or two" (Grafton 1982, 308). V. I. Warshawski is never really okay and so we'll turn to her now.

3.1 Sara Parektsky: Anger's Power and Privilege

Vic is one of the most explicitly angry female detectives ever. Her creator, Sara Paretsky, has never backed away from feminist anger in twenty-two (and counting) novels, short stories, nonfiction writing, and interviews. Vic shows us anger's many iterations, from red-hot righteousness to the traumatic wound speaking its exhausted name; nevertheless, anger and justice remain inextricably linked. Vic says, in *Bitter Medicine*, "I had to be angry with someone" (Paretsky 2021: 35). As the "someone" indicates, anger in Paretsky is also complicated. While there are clear targets and particular investigations in each novel, there is also a lot of ambient anger in Paretsky's work and frequent harm to her inner circle. The abuse of power within families, sometimes resolved, is

---

[33] Grafton 1982: 37.

linked to the abuse of power within institutions, practically never resolved. There are no psycho serial killers or "bad apples" in Paretsky – most lives are shaped by structural violence – but there are chronic winners and losers, and Vic's anger motivates her to play David to corrupt corporate America's Goliath. Since *Indemnity Only* first appeared in 1982, all the books have woven together individual crimes with broader social issues, including (but very much not limited to): political and financial corruption, reproductive rights, censorship, health care inequities, nuclear proliferation, gentrification, gun violence, and the criminalization of the poor. Paretsky's long-running series explores both the power of anger as a tool for social justice and its collateral damage.

Vic's anger is partly a reflection of her creator's life experience. Cynthia S. Hamilton explores Paretsky's biography in relation to the novels and Paretsky's political commitments.[34] Paretsky, who has an MBA and PhD in history from the University of Chicago, uses the genre to chart the false promises of American society. Her *Writing in the Age of Silence* is a collection of essays written partly in response to post-9/11 US politics:

> I cannot find the words to express the depth of my loss or my outrage, to see my country abrogate treaties abroad, and violate the very heart and bones of our Constitution here at home. Some of us feel corrupt and tainted, others weak and angry, and the mood of the country is ugly. As a writer, in a time like this, it is hard to know what to say and how to say it. (Paretsky 2007: 111)

Blacklist (2004) is set in the wake of the Trade Center attack. The fitness-conscious Vic has lost ten pounds in the six months after 9/11. Her friend Dr. Lotty Herschel says she "was fine physically, just suffering as so many were from exhaustion of the spirit" (Paretsky 2004: 3). Paretsky believes the private eye is a crusader: "In our nation's mythology, honorable people have to take the law into their own hands to preserve fundamental, immutable Justice. This is Justice with a capital J because justice with a small j has been bought and perverted by the powerful" (Paretsky 2007: 104). Like Hopkins, Paretsky places America's unfinished business with justice at the center of female-centered crime fiction. In the recent *Pay Dirt* (2024), Paretsky makes this point by taking Vic's investigation back, like Hopkins, to Civil War–era crimes.

---

[34] Paretsky's feminism has been a source of scholarly debate over the past three decades. Sally Munt (*Murder by the Book*; Munt's book is 1994), Andrew Pepper is 2000 (*The Contemporary American Crime Novel: Race, Ethnicity, Gender, Class*), and Gil Plain is (*Twentieth-Century Crime Fiction: Gender, Sexuality and the Body*) see Paretsky's politics as compromised by the blind spots of second-wave feminism and liberalism. Priscilla L. Walton and Jones is 1999 (*Detective Agency: Women Rewriting the Hard-boiled Tradition*) and Cynthia S. Hamilton (*Sara Paretsky: Detective Fiction as Trauma Literature*; 2021) see Paretsky as successfully navigating conservative aspects of the detective fiction formula as well as being marked by the complicated positions of a feminism that has evolved over several decades.

Anger is mentioned in the first chapters of almost every Warshawski novel. There are simply too many instances to mention, but what is notable is how full-bodied and volatile Vic's anger is. In *Bitter Medicine* (1987), the powers that be want to move a friend of Vic's, a young, pregnant working-class Mexican woman, to a public hospital. "I could feel my head vibrating with rage," she explains. "I thought the top of my head would come off and it was all I could do to keep from seizing [the receptionist] and smashing her face" (Paretsky 2021: 13). In *Blacklist*, Vic wants to "hurl a bazooka rocket" through the window of a rich woman who is obstructing her investigation, "something that would make an explosion big enough to match my impotent fury" (Paretsky 2004: 380). A friend and former lover explains that "Vic favors the Dick Butkus approach to detection – hit the offense hard ... then see who's left on the ground when she gets done. If you're looking for Sherlock Holmes or Nero Wolfe doing some fancy intellectual footwork, forget it" (Paretsky 2021: 260). At times, she comes close to the Nussbaum line, where anger inevitably descends into revenge. She frequently wonders about her motivations regarding her ex-husband Dick, "the very picture of affluent power" (Paretsky 2021: 295), whose continual appearance throughout the series reminds us that the working-class Vic gave up a life of privilege because she wasn't willing to be "a good girl" (Paretsky 2021: 139). In *Bitter Medicine*, Dick is representing the antichoice activists who trashed Lotty's clinic: "I was very angry, certainly ... but would I have been as hot on the trail if some other attorney had represented him? I hated to think I suffered from residual bitterness after all these years" (Paretsky 2021: 152). But later, at a courtroom press conference, she wants to grab a mike and bash his brains out (Paretsky 2021: 296). In *Tunnel Vision*, a friend calls her "a progressive Dirty Harry" (Paretsky 1994: 13).

But as much as giving into her violent instincts might make her day, Vic is also shown controlling them. In *Tunnel Vision*, she gets grilled by a cop and "a fireball of anger swept through me. I jammed my hands into my jeans pockets to keep from leaping over the table to punch him. No one ever got anywhere hitting a cop" (Paretsky 1994: 104). We see here that Vic both feels rage but also understands the importance of regulating it in her quest for justice. As she pursues corporate corruption through two homes broken by domestic violence, "anger started to build inside me [and] the back of my head began to pound. Easy does it, I admonished myself. Getting angry only made you careless" (Paretsky 1994: 296). In *Blacklist*, she reminds herself that "I needed my wits, not my emotions, for whatever lay ahead" (Paretsky 2004: 432). In *Fallout*, "I had my temper on a lead as tight as the one I'd kept on Peppy," one of her beloved golden retrievers (Paretsky 2017: 136).

Most Paretsky novels contain an aside, a small plot point mentioned by a minor character, illustrating that not everyone does rein in their anger. A social worker tells Vic that "we had a woman here for a while, she's doing ten years now, who poured lye on her old man while he was asleep, then coated him with molasses. He burned to death – he couldn't wash the stuff off. She was four-foot-eleven. The courts didn't care that she only had one major limb the guy hadn't broken" (Paretsky 1994: 158). Stories like this illustrate the barely contained seething that shapes female lives under patriarchy, and provide a context both for Vic's anger and its control as well as the collateral damage experienced by those in her world. A recurring aspect of the Warshawski books is that her beloved found family – including Viennese refugee, mother figure, and doctor, Lotty Herschel, and her elderly downstairs neighbor, Mr. Contreras, with whom she coparents her dogs – are often harmed because of her work. When "some thugs mistook Lotty for me and broke her arm," Vic explains, her "anger and my remorse had cut a channel between us that we rebridged only after months of hard work. Every now and then it gapes open again" (Paretsky 1994: 15–16). Mr. Contreras has been hospitalized more than once for involving himself in Vic's work. When Vic comes home in *Bitter Medicine* to find her apartment broken into and Mr. Contreras unconscious, she experiences "anger, shock, the goddamned fucking last straw" (Paretsky 2021: 175).

She lives her life holding that last straw and it makes her cynical: "But we would all pretend that the burglary squad's fingerprinting and searching would really accomplish something" (Paretsky 2021: 176). And weary: "I'm tired. I spent a month risking my life for some abstract concept of justice, and all that happened in the end was my lover left me" (Paretsky 1994: 460). But Vic's anger, while exhausting, also motivates: "Action. What every detective needs" (Paretsky 2021: 182). In *Blacklist*, when she has to dive into a pool to find a dead body, "self-pitying tears spurted out. I dashed them away angrily. You're a woman saved by action, I mocked myself: get the damned fins on and get going" (Paretsky 2004: 201). When she is trapped in a missile silo in *Fallout*, she's asked by her companion "We're trapped, aren't we? We're going to die here?" Vic thinks that "Cady's dull, helpless tone so echoed my own mood that I became angry. These men are not going to manage our fate the way they did Doris McKinnon's or Dr. Roque's" (women whose lives and careers were ended by patriarchal ass-covering). "We will survive and thrive," I said fiercely (Paretsky 2017: 401).

Vic shares with the hard-boiled hero a problematic individualism, one of the second-wave limitations critics find with her and other strong women sleuths. She knows she became "a private eye because I wanted to be my own boss" (Paretsky 1994: 43) and that she uses, in Lotty's words, "anger or fear to put up walls between [herself] and other people" (Paretsky 1994: 291). Lotty also routinely takes her to task for assuming too much authority over people's lives: "you just can't continue to set your own judgment up as God's in these kinds of situations" (Paretsky 1994: 34). Throughout the novels, Paretsky reflects on the power struggles of women's lives, which are messier than Vic's own bravado would like to acknowledge. We see this, as well, in the representation of trauma in the novels. In practically every novel, Vic is physically assaulted, often accompanied by the threat of sexual violence. In *Bitter Medicine*, Sergio, a gangster and Vic's aggrieved former client from her public defender days, says, "'I don't want to ruin you in case you ever get a man, Warshawki, so I'm just going to leave a little reminder.' He took out a knife" (Paretsky 2021: 68). Vic acknowledges the trauma; after Sergio's attack, she "knew I should get to a doctor ... but a vast lethargy enveloped me. All I wanted to do was go to bed and never get up again. Never try again to – to do anything" (Paretsky 2021: 69). It affects her memory, and losses in these novels evoke other losses. We learn about her mother's death when she was a teenager: "My own mother's death had been the cataclysmic event of my life. In some ways I don't think I've ever recovered from it" (Parestky 2021: 113–114). While these are things that happen to Vic personally, potentially isolating her, these novels work to show how trauma connects women in a world that takes such life cheaply.

In this way, Paretsky pays attention to victims and the retraumatizing injustices the legal system visits upon them, a commitment of feminist crime fiction. Hamilton's full-length study of Paretsky credits her with using "the narrative structure of the detective story to condemn those totalising narratives of history that would exclude and silence the marginalised and the victimised" (Hamilton 2021: 1). Paretsky's villains are greedy, products of a rapacious and corrupting capitalism. Compared to the detailed portraits of psychopathy and serial killers that one might find in, for example, Patricia Cornwell, Paretsky's villains are banal. But her victims are vividly portrayed. She tries to represent their complex experiences. When an emotionally and sexually abused daughter refuses to speak, the doctor thinks she had "a psychotic breakdown," but Vic says she "could just be too angry to want to talk to any more adults at this point" (Paretsky 1994: 329). This young woman is ultimately helped by a female cop who shares her experience of abuse and the retraumatization of the system: "I joined the force because I wanted to arrest creeps like my father ... But now, instead of arresting the creep, I'm supposed to arrest the kid. It's like they want me to send myself to jail. Or worse, to a mental hospital where a girl like Emily will have on chance in a thousand of coming out with her head straight" (Paretsky 1994: 383–384). Vic tries to explain what seems to be irrational behavior as a trauma response: "That's a real problem for women in violent households. They know if they fight back when the man's assaulting them they're going to be hurt really badly. So they withdraw – emotionally – from the scene. It's only later that they can feel the anger" (Paretsky 1994: 169).

Sometimes cynic, sometimes loner, Vic nevertheless sees her work as a kind of care. She writes to musician boyfriend, Jake, who'd hoped she'd leave detective work to follow him around Europe, "I have my own mission on the planet. It isn't as beautiful or ennobling as music, but I also heal people's lives" (Paretsky 2017: 234). As Cady, a young woman whose familial mystery is intertwined with dark secrets from the US nuclear arms race, climbs out of the missile silo in *Fallout*, Vic follows her up the stairs, "patting her legs after each rung: you're not alone, keep going" (Paretsky 2017: 409). It's a pep talk Paretsky gives herself sometimes. She writes in *Writing in an Age of Silence*, "I'm still doing feminism. And so is my detective, V. I. Warshawski. We are both dogged, even if we can't keep up with modern fashions" (Paretsky 2007: 77). She is inspired by her community of readers:

> They came to my lecture to tell me that the blue-collar girl detective helped them get through this very difficult hand that life had dealt them. So although my words are only water squeezed from a rock, and although there are many days where I feel as though my voice, my very self were being crushed beneath that rock, these women have told me to get up, sit down, and keep writing. (Paretsky 2007: 77–78)

And she does. But part of the problem with the twenty-two-plus book series is that the attachment to justice, saving a world that needs to be saved again and again (to paraphrase Theodore Martin), can read like cruel optimism. This creates the kind of inauthentic closure we saw in *Lady Audley's Secret*. At the end of most novels, Paretsky throws the reader a bone (or, in the case of *Bitter Medicine*, a stick for Peppy, hurled into the lake). For example, *Tunnel Vision*, a novel full of awful domestic abuse, ends with a surprise birthday party for Vic, in which "champagne flowed like water, and we danced until the pale moon sank" (Paretsky 1994: 464). Even though closure is not commensurate with justice, narrative resolution, long seen as a conservative aspect of the detective genre, is a kind of privilege. As we saw with the muted endings of female-centered crime fiction in the previous section, lack of closure both marks injustice and holds space for justice to be done in the future. The endings read as waiting rather than resolution. Hamilton considers Paretsky's "ambivalences ... shared by many of her generation" which reflect "the shifting agendas between second and third wave feminism and the challenges these posed for women who sought to claim, redefine, or eschew the feminist label" (Hamilton 2021: 7).

We see shifting feminist agendas in Denise Mina's Alex Morrow series (2009–), which is both working in and against the Paretsky tradition. Detective Inspector Morrow is angry, and, as one of the few females in a Glasgow police department, isolated. She is also isolated by her own personal trauma. But Mina decenters Alex's individual experience by having her story as one of several in each novel's interwoven narratives of crime and, occasionally, justice. Mina also increasingly attempts, over the course of the series, to have Alex act more from a place of love than from anger. This is how we first meet Morrow in *Still Midnight*: "Alex Morrow bit slowly into her index finger, pressing her teeth until she could hear a small crunch in the skin. She was so angry that the upper lid of her left eye was twitching, blurring the changing view through the rain-splattered car window" (Mina 2009: 21). Mina begins with Alex as a classic angry female dick, with trouble at home (the loss of a child has strained her marriage), trouble in the past that threatens the present (she comes from a broken, working-class home, and her brother, Danny, is a powerful drug dealer in town), and difficulty negotiating squad politics ("she knew her anger was disproportionate and scattered, leaking from her like water through a sock"; Mina 2009: 22). In the second novel, *The End of the Wasp Season*, Alex is pregnant again, but she is using her anger: "anger was her trump card, the sole emotion that could sweep sorrow to the curb. Stay angry, stay detached" (Mina 2011: 38). Alex uses her anger as a source of regulating *other* ugly feelings (shame, grief, fear). Such feelings are shared by and form a bond with her brother: "she could see herself in him utterly, deep-rooted fear making him angry, wanting to control the desperate, craven desire to belong" (Mina 2009: 323). They both have been shaped by their traumatic childhood: their "mother's anger had colored her whole life" (Mina 2014: 125).

But over the course of the (at the time of this writing) five books of the series, Mina is also exploring how a working-class angry dick might work through it. In the third novel, *Gods and Beasts*, Morrow is happier, the new mother of twin boys. In a published conversation with the author appended to *Gods and Beasts*, Mina explains that she "wanted to counter all of those cliches" of the angry, hard-drinking loner detective "with a well-functioning woman who loves her man and her home" (Mina 2014). Mina's novels are more decentered than those with first-person sleuths. Alex's story, told in the third person, is only one of the viewpoints in the novels, and we often spend as much (if not more) time with the perpetrators and victims. As Mina explains, "I wanted to take a more holistic view of a crime and spend time with the criminals, police and victims so they're kind of short stories that intersect through the events in the first chapter ... Criminology nowadays tends to look at crime as an event produced by a system, rather than one person doing something" (Mina 2014). Justice is often not done, and Morrow knows it: "For Morrow, the cases that kept her burning eyes blinking into the dark were not the bloody ones, not the vicious ones when eyes were gouged or fingers snapped or children hurt. Morrow's keepers were those where events seemed inevitable, the cases that made her doubt the possibility of justice" (Mina 2011: 211). The world of the police force is as corrupt as organized crime, the linkage between the two worlds embodied in her sibling relationship. At the end of *Gods and Beasts*, an innocent woman is brutally raped in her home by enforcers working for Danny, whom Alex has just invited to be a godfather to her twins. The anger of white female sleuths, while directed toward structural violence, whether on the streets of Chicago or Glasgow, and often lacking resolution, is nevertheless a kind of privilege, and not available to non-white characters in the same way.

3.2 Barbara Neely and the Legacy of Intersectional Anger

Blanche White appeared on the scene about a decade after Millhone and Warshawski, but is a recognizable series sleuth from the first chapter. Blanche feels her feelings as strongly as Vic, but the reader gets them in the third person, rather than Paretsky's use of the first person (this is even more complicated when we get to the second-person narration of Lauren Wilkinson's *American Spy*). Is Neely implying that the first-person privileges of the strong-woman genre, such as the public display of anger, are less available to Black women like Blanche? Might the third person more directly locate Blanche in a community, essential to who Blanche is and what she does? Rebecca Traister notes how "the cultural caricature of neck-snapping, side-eye-casting black female" anger is embraced for its humor which then serves to disconnect it from "real political, economic, or social power" (Traister 2018: 77). Neely's sleuth drives a mack truck over this caricature. She is not without the side eye, or the funny zinger, but every line Neely writes is connected to a vital understanding of power. In the four novels that constitute the Blanche White series, Neely joins Paretsky in making the crime novel about the imbrication between personal and political violence. But her Black female rage has its own journey through what it means to "use it." The first Blanche White novel, *Blanche on the Lam* (1992), finds Neely's sleuth, a Black domestic worker, back in the South of her childhood. Blanche is the spiritual heir of Henny and Venus. Neely maintains Hopkins's use of the crime story as a way to expose continued American injustice, from the perspective of a Black woman who can look back on both the promise and the failures of Civil Rights movements, who finds promise in the strong female agency of the series detective, and yet who stands in a different relationship to American injustice than her white sisters. Blanche has what Brittney Cooper calls "sass" – a "more palatable form of rage" that negotiates between justice and self-preservation. As Blanche says, "This is how we've survived in this country all this time, by knowing when to act like we believe what we've been told and when to act like we know what we know" (Neely 1992: 73).

Hopkins has a courtroom scene toward the end of her novel; Neely starts there. But Blanche is not – even ninety years later – the important witness, or even a lawyer, but rather the accused: she finds herself sentenced to "thirty days and restitution" for a bounced check (Neely 1992: 1). The courtroom is still a place where extrajudicial violence is possible: when Blanche is being taken away by the matron, she "looked around the courtroom, but no one was interested enough to look back ... A dark blond, bullet-headed boy in jeans and cowboy boots sat on a long bench against the wall ... Blanche tried to catch the boy's eye, to see and be seen by someone before they both disappeared into ... She clutched her stomach and half turned to the matron" (Neely 1992: 2). We know Neely means disappearing into jail, but the sentence is finished by Blanche's dodgy bowels. "I gotta use the toilet!" she announces and, in one pointed and funny paragraph, the courtroom is replaced by the restroom. Blanche plots her escape on the toilet ... and refuses to flush.

Blanche is not without her fears as she buys herself time to figure out her situation. But anger is what gives her strength (if not clarity). Right before she flees, she thinks she "should be convincing herself that she could and would survive the next thirty days. Instead she raged at the judge for being an unfair dickbrain" (Neely 1992: 3). As she hides out while doing temp work for a rich white family who "thought they were still living in slavery days, when a black woman was grateful for the chance to work indoors" (Neely 1992: 4), she learns of a plot to cheat Mumsfield, a young family member with mosaic Down syndrome. As she pokes around while cooking meals, and slyly spits on Civil War monuments (Neely 1992: 75) while doing errands, the bodycount mounts. Blanche looks for chances to get away, to save herself without necessarily solving the larger mystery: she isn't sure what "justice" for this family has to do with her, other than a nagging sense of kinship with Mumsfield whose "condition made him as invisible as her color and profession made her" (Neely 1992: 103). Unlike Vic, Blanche isn't serving a client, and unlike Morrow, Blanche is not a cop. But, like them, her anger, entwined with her working-class identity, connects her to a broader sense of justice. When Nate, the Black gardener, is killed, Blanche is transformed:

> a thick, hot rage began to roil in her stomach at the thought of the deaths of all the poor black Nates and, yes, Blanches ... Men like Nate and women like her were the people, the folks, the mud from which the rest were made. It was

their hands and blood and sweat that had built everything, from the North Carolina governor's mansion to the first stoplight. They ought to have been appreciated for being the wattle that held the walls together. Instead, they were expendable, interchangeable, rarely missed, hardly regarded, easily forgotten. Not this time! (Neely 1992: 149)

She considers her next move, and "the fiery rage in her belly and the ice encasing her heart made her unfit for human companionship" (Neely 1992: 151). Blanche is the female detective as latter-day Fury.

In fighting for the little guy against structural violence, Blanche continues the work of feminist sleuths like Vic. But in a move that reflects the racial fault lines of second-wave feminism, Neely makes the novel's main criminal a privileged white woman: Grace, Blanche's temporary employer. Blanche herself is surprised that the perpetrator of a string of crimes is not the handsome white Southern gentleman but rather his seemingly dotty wife, and is "shocked and frightened" when it dawns on her, "a person whose living depended on her ability to read character" (Neely 1992: 184). As the truth comes out, we learn that Grace has exhibited sociopathic tendencies since childhood days, but has not been held accountable, able to move through social space protected by her privilege. Unlike Blanche, who must slow her post-court-house run because a "running black person was still a target of suspicion in this town, even if the runner was a woman" (Neely 1992: 6). Neely's message is clear: race trumps gender in the ways bodies are understood, and an unquestioning gender solidarity can be dangerous.

Black maid sleuths and a critique of the American legal system are not the only things Neely continues from the stories of Hopkins. At the heart of *Blanche on the Lam* is a passing story. The inheritance plot depends on the kidnapping of an elderly rich cousin and substituting a look-alike, a distant relation, who is the offspring of the great uncle and a domestic worker. The discovery of this secret leads to Nate's murder, as the killer explains: "How was I to know Nate would recognize her? They say you people always know one of your own, no matter how light-skinned. But she was so white . . . " (Neely 1992: 194). Though Nate recognizes her and Blanche doesn't, giving the lie to the racist "you people always know" idea, the problem of passing again unsettles the operations of justice: the cousin is murdered, the substitute disappears, and there is no real justice offered for these particular characters. Like Hopkins, Neely resists providing closure. The novel ends with Blanche on the move: "she had no place else to go – at least to make a living – except among those who disdained her to death" (Neely 1992: 215). As the first in a series, storylines obviously have to be kept open, but it is more than that. The crimes Blanche solves stem from the unfinished business of American justice: indeed, the next book in the series, *Blanche Among the Talented Tenth*, tackles colorism within the Black community, among folks who, like Talma Gordon's fiancé, can stand accusations of murder but recoil at too much "Negro blood."

The final novel in the series, *Blanche Passes Go*, finds the sleuth still angry. In the first chapters, she fights off unwanted sexual advances on behalf of a coworker; the rage over "this piece of black women's old race knowledge" smells to her "like hair burning" (Neely 2000: 23). The long story of sexual assault is personal for Blanche, as she returns to the South again where she will have to figure out what to do with her anger: "Over the years, as time and distance forged scar tissue tough enough to dull the pain of what he'd done to her, thoughts of revenge had faded, too. But there would be little distance between them now" (Neely 2000: 6). As Blanche sorts through her own feelings and stumbles into another mystery, she is surrounded by women who have also been assaulted and feels "a tug on the chain of harmed women" (Neely 2000: 43). The story is about finding "a way to fight back" (Neely 2000: 34), and explores how anger can manifest in justice, but also in self-harm and revenge. Blanche wonders if maybe "she would be able to bring her own attacker to something that at least passed for payback, if not for justice" (Neely 2000: 111). She worries that she could get lost in her anger: "this was the kind of shit that made a person sick" (Neely 2000: 44), whereas she wants to see "herself in the center of a forward-moving life" (Neely 2000: 49).

Blanche shares the hard-boiled hero's dilemma, shuttling between the support of her community, such as best friend Ardell, elder Miz Minnie, and the Ancestors who are always with her, and a commitment to her own autonomy. In this final novel, she is "fifty and free" (Neely 2000: 11), and "her own priest and goddess" (Neely 2000: 12). As Lotty warned V. I., Blanche is warned by an old neighbor: "There's the kind of taking care of yourself that's about keeping yourself together, and there's the kind that's about keeping other people away from yourself. It ain't so smart to get them confused" (Neely 2000: 153). Sisterhood is fraught for Blanche. She did not want children, but she is raising her dead sister's kids and is passionately attached to them. She wonders from time to time if her sister made her their guardian as a kind of punishment for Blanche's quest for freedom. Blanche knows sisterhood is not easy, but also that it is a crucial part of moving forward. Blanche and her female neighbors confront an abuser across the street: "Maybe the only way to end this mess was for every woman to stand up for every other woman, even if she couldn't stand up for herself" (Neely 2000: 320). Predictably, the abuser plays the crazy card: "All you bitches is crazy!" Blanche takes a step back – "one more bit of rage would surely burn her alive" – but she does give the woman the name of a shelter (Neely 2000: 320).

Justice for the Black female detective is complicated in part because, as Blanche explains, we "all played a part in this mess, but we ain't all equally responsible" (Neely 2000: 315). The ending of this series is muted rather than triumphant. When Blanche's rapist dies as a consequence of her investigation, she thinks she "didn't want him alive so that his life could go merrily along, or even so that she'd have another chance to try to bring him down. She wanted him alive so that she wouldn't have to carry the weight of knowing she was partly responsible for his death, no matter how light the load" (Neely 2000: 316). In "Thinking with Character," Amanda Anderson explores "rumination" as a kind of moral thinking that, like anger, is "often the result of intensely felt injustice" and can register commitment to social critique (Anderson, Felski, & Moi 2019: 137). A sense of injustice paired with quasi-obsessive thinking is the detective's métier, but rumination doesn't necessarily lead to any particular action. Part of the structures of seething, rumination bides its time. Blanche's quest for justice requires ruminating on accountability, which keeps her from reactive payback, but doesn't hurtle her forward into a fairy-tale future.[35] The series ends as it begins, somewhat circularly, with us waiting for Blanche to make up her mind between a series of suboptimal choices. She doesn't want to remain in the South, can't wait to get out of "that racist Boston," and New York "made Boston look good" (Neely 2000: 321). The series ends with Blanche on the porch, watching the woman across the street pack up to move with her daughters to the shelter.

Contemporary crime fighters of color have picked up where Blanche left off, using anger to solve mysteries and right social wrongs, but also standing at an angle to white anger's privileges. Juniper Song is the LA-based sleuth of three novels by Steph Cha. Song is solidly using it, but also providing a Korean-American lens on issues facing the strong female character, illustrating that intersections of race, gender, class, and immigration status can shape the expression of anger. The first novel, *Follow Her Home* (2013), is the most personal, and we learn that Song, like most female sleuths, has a traumatic backstory in the suicide of her sister. As it was for Blanche, the missing sister is a symbol of Song's challenges in finding female solidarity as a solution to injustice. Song's family background also illustrates how immigrants are additionally vulnerable to injustice, sometimes blurring the legal line in order to meet their needs and those of their communities. The second novel, Beware *Beware* (2014), finds her working as an apprentice at a PI firm and living in a fog of trauma with Lori from the first novel. By the third, *Dead Soon Enough* (2015),

---

[35] Anderson embraces "rumination" as a messy feeling rather than seeing it simply as an obsessive or "maladaptive" practice.

Song is a junior partner. Song is obsessed with Raymond Chandler's Philip Marlowe, and shares the hard-drinking, the violence, and ultimately being "part of the nastiness" (Chandler 1992: 230). Her anger is less evident than Warshawski's, Morrow's, or Neely's, manifesting more in hard-boiled quips and as much tough guy swagger as her lanky 5'9" frame, and the TASER in her glove compartment, can convey. But she is also in conversation with the larger history of crime narrative beyond Chandler. Like Paretsky, Cha sees individual crime as linked to structural violence; Song feels what Blanche called the "tug on the chain of harmed women." But as a Korean-American millennial, her anger and her outlook on justice are shaped by her particular cultural location.

The first novel, *Follow Her Home*, is filled with violence, but a first reading might make you miss that Song is angry about it. She is not intimidating, as she explains in a later novel: "Being an Asian woman worked in my favor – despite my height and somewhat unforthcoming demeanor, no one ever thought I was dangerous" (Cha 2015: 10). In Beware *Beware*, Song admits that she "was good at hiding emotions" (Cha 2014: 129). Cha shows us how women's anger blurs with other more socially acceptable, if uncomfortable, feelings: "A quick burn of anger flushed through me, and it was tinged with humiliation" (Cha, 2014: 168); later, "though he was making me angry, what I felt most was embarrassment" (Cha 2014: 171). It isn't until chapter 8 of the first novel that Song distinguishes herself from hard-boiled cool: "I was no Marlowe. Where he was ever composed and competent, I moved in response to jolts of love and fury" (Cha 2013: 121). Like Warshawski and Blanche, she feels this viscerally. Hearing about the murder of her friend and former boyfriend, she "felt whiteness scar the backs of my eyes, dizzying and hot" (Cha 2013: 252). Rage is frequently felt behind her eyes, as if to signal that it shapes the way she sees things. She imagines using violence against a reluctant witness: "I imagined getting up from my chair and smacking him. I heard the bright, dry sound of it echo in my head, felt the phantom sting heat up my palm . . . I was going to break him down" (Cha 2014: 209). Song is overwhelmed by her feelings in the second novel. She discovers that her client has been the victim of multiple rapes, including by a Hollywood superstar, and this dramatically reframes things for her. When Song is invited to downplay this detail by the star's personal assistant – "I mean he didn't *rape* rape her" – Song's "head filled with heat and I had a hard time controlling my voice: 'The fuck does that mean?'" (Cha 2014: 185). She storms out "in [a] righteous rage, and the heat of it welded the door shut" (Cha 2014: 186). She "feels a short jolt of vicious satisfaction, and thought about revenge" (Cha 2014: 197), but acknowledges that she needs to regulate her feelings to keep future doors open. As if to underscore the risks to women of losing it, the next novel, *Dead Soon Enough*, begins with a missing woman,

Nora, an Armenian activist whose final blog post is a response to the violently misogynist trolls who post "rape threats on the daily": "listen up, you horde of disgusting anonymous cum wads: Enough is enough. I'm coming for you" (Cha, 2015: 25). Nora's fiancé tells Song that if his missing girlfriend had "stayed in law school, kept herself quiet, no one would have had any reason to hurt her" (Cha 2015: 75).

The second and third novels in particular broaden the focus on crime to include systemic violence. Beware *Beware* can be read as a rape-revenge narrative. When Song asks Daphne, her client in the novel, if she knows "that kind of man" who will do anything to get what he wants, "She shot me a bitter smile. 'Everyone does, Song. Every last one of us'" (Cha 2014: 130). The victim becomes the aggressor in this novel; Daphne is depicted as a femme fatale: "she was angry, burning and dangerous" (Cha 2014: 281). But she is also justified and sane, "not a crazy bitch" (Cha 2014: 290). Daphne has been raped three times; "rape is about as common as disaster can get," she explains, and "here's something else fucked up: Once you get raped, you're more likely to get raped again. It's like biting your tongue" (Cha 2014: 263–264). Daphne's explanation for how she embarks on a series of premeditated murders was that she "was so angry. You can't imagine how angry" (Cha 2014: 218). Song can imagine; she is the victim of attempted rape toward the end of the novel. As she recovers from being roofied, "rage displaced some of the drowsiness vying for my body" (Cha 2014: 252). Like Blanche, she connects with a long women's history of sexual violence and, like Blanche, she regulates herself: "I thought I might cry then, felt the motion of hurt and disgust roil deep inside of me, ancient, permanent, and profound. But I didn't. I willed myself to stay calm, to yield my emotions to the balm of shock, and to take stock of the scene instead" (Cha 2014: 255). In the third novel, which focuses on contemporary struggles to remember and memorialize the Armenian genocide, Song also identifies with a broader experience of violence and the transgenerational anger it engenders. Song reveals that her great aunt was a comfort woman in World War II. "I get it, by the way. The historical anger . . . I know what it's like to feel rage in my blood" (Cha 2015: 109).

Like Vic and Blanche, Song's rage is partly mitigated by a supportive community. Not only her friend Lori, but also her bosses at the agency are both mentors and quasi-family. She also forms an alliance with detective Vanessa Sanchez of the LAPD, a lesbian who takes a liking to Song even as she is wary of being used by her. While Song understands that part of her work is to provide care for those who are vulnerable, she initially sees her connection to Marlowe through the lens of justice: "It might have been this impulse that led me to private detection in the first place – the Marlowe drive, the itchy longing to uncover ugly soil, to dislodge the bad fruit that rooted below" (Cha 2014: 217). She is also bonded to Marlowe in both the cover up and the resulting exhaustion: "I was part of the nastiness now, another cheap asshole willing to shoulder her share of corruption" (Cha 2014: 285). She sanctions Daphne's extrajudicial killing as a kind of justice and doesn't turn her in. In the third novel, she decides to spare her client further suffering by concealing what she knows about the murder. Missing bodies stay missing, and Song "could feel the madness around this uncertainty" (Cha 2015: 227). The novels end on an uneasy note, with uncertainty all around, for women, for immigrants, for underresourced youth. Song says that she's "seen so much death in the last week, I feel like I'm in a fucking Greek tragedy" (Cha 2014: 274). Song is contained, ultimately more Kindly One than Fury. But she ends the final novel troubling the surface of the Underworld: "I tore up a handful of grass and scattered it back on the ground. 'It is what it is, I guess. Might as well get used to it'" (Cha 2015: 292).

No one knows that "it is what it is" like a Black woman from Detroit. Cheryl A. Head's Charlene "Charlie" Mack has much in common with the sleuths in this section: anger about injustice motivates her work. But Head's novels (six so far) also reframe some of the issues around individualism, intersectionality, anger, and justice in ways that offer alternatives to messy feelings. Mack is a character still figuring things out, having been a small business owner, an immigration agent with Homeland Security, and now the head of her own private investigations team. Being part of a team decenters her authority, challenging some of the individualism of the hard-boiled sleuth; as Head explains, the "four-person agency bore Charlie's name because she was the principal investor. But things were actually much more egalitarian ... The agency's success was built on their diverse experience, networks and mutual respect for each other" (Head 2018: 7). These novels, told in the third person, are more akin to police procedurals, which emphasize the business of detective work. Rare glimpses of emotion are thrown into relief. In addition to building her agency, Charlie is also exploring her sexual orientation (she was previously married to a man and is now in a relationship with a woman) and caring for a mother with Alzheimer's, a poignant disease for a PI daughter, given that its symptoms involve both anger and forgetting. Head puts Charlie in a complex emotional ecosystem, and puts crimes in complex histories of violence. The first mystery, *Bury Me When I'm Dead*, takes her back to the South, which holds history not only for her but for her Mexican-American partner, linking histories of slavery and immigration – another way that Head, like Cha, reframes our understanding of the subjects of American injustice. But they don't have to go to the South for this: Mack, a Detroit-based PI, lives in a city with a long history of racism and economic precarity, and where streets are named "after dead white men from Detroit's past" (Head, 2016: 5). The second novel, *Wake Me When It's*

Over, set in the years following 9/11, addresses broader questions of terrorism. Charlie's girlfriend, Mandy, lost a brother on that day and tells Charlie that "even after four years, I'm angry about 9/11. I think about it almost every day" (Head 2018: 23). Charlie understands, but also points out that "we've had terrorism in this country since the Revolutionary War. Only the form has changed" (Head 2018: 23). Later in the story, a Black woman working with the Mack team says "I'm glad that Mack woman is in charge of this. Because in America, I know black people have way more experience with terrorism than white people" (Head 2018: 112).

When we first meet Charlie she is angry. Asked to provide a second piece of identification to make a deposit, ("*Deposit*, mind you"), "anger sprouted in the pit of her stomach" and she works to slow "the rise of her blood pressure" (Head 2016: 4). Later in the novel, she confronts some clients who have been keeping a secret and her "anger was an explosion" (Head 2016: 233). But the third-person narration holds these characters at a bit of a remove, and so we hear about her anger from the perspective of her partner: "Don studied Charlie's posture. Her hands were clenched at her sides. He'd seen her this angry before when someone took advantage of innocents. The last time, she'd laid out a child molester so quickly the man didn't have a chance to even think about running" (Head 2016: 233). When a young colleague is kidnapped by Heinrich, one of the villains in *Wake Me When It's Over*, a "dark feeling came over Charlie." She tells Mandy that she was "thinking about killing Heinrich" as payback (Head 2018: 137).

So while she is capable of doing harm – Charlie is a fourth-degree black belt, and her partner Gil says "you really don't want to make her mad" (Head 2018: 136) – Head is all about being productive. She tells Mandy that as "an adult I've been careful to avoid situations where I couldn't control my circumstances or at least protect myself. That's driven most of the decisions I've ever made" (Head 2016: 193). In the second novel, she comforts Mandy after the death of a colleague, Josh; she admits that she, too, "was angry and stunned, but I wouldn't allow myself to think about my grief. I made sure to get money for Josh's family, but I haven't shed one tear for him" (Head 2018: 108). Charlie holds it together and stays focused on "her sense of justice," clearer in Head than in the other works. "I like to think that all my work has been about helping people" (Head 2016: 189).

Lauren Wilkinson weaves questions of anger, intersectional identity, and justice into the spy novel. Her 2018 *American Spy* is set in the 1980s (with flashbacks to scenes in the 1960s), so it looks back at important moments in America's sense of itself while also being two years into the Trump presidency. Wilkinson asks what happens when we take our barely passing justice, and our seething sleuth, and export them worldwide? Marie Mitchell, the main character, is a Black female FBI intelligence officer committed to a career fighting for justice. She is also looking for a chance to accelerate her career, and is very angry at the sexism and racism that is sidelining her (she is routinely decried for not being a "team player"), at her Martinican mother who left her as a child, at her Black American policeman father who raised her in New York, and at her dead sister, an Army intelligence rookie who had "an unusual capacity for rage" (Wilkinson 2018: 59) and left behind a lot of unanswered questions. She is also becoming angry at the United States, a country which views Black liberation and communism in the same threatening vein.

Marie gets a career break when she is invited by the CIA to be a temporary contractor in order to get close to Thomas Sankara during his visit to the United Nations in 1984. Sankara, the real-life president of Burkina-Faso until his assassination in 1987, is initially threatening to Marie. As a cop's daughter and nuke-fearing child of the Cold War, she is not a fan of radicals. And she is ambitious, so she accepts the CIA position and embarks on a journey that will find her learning more about American foreign policy, traveling to Africa, and ultimately making her own decisions about what is just. And it is not American democracy: when told that the CIA wants to overthrow Sankara's government to create a multiparty system "because a multiparty system is a basic element of democracy," Marie responds "it's an odd agenda for the CIA to have when *our* government isn't a multiparty system" (Wilkinson 2018: 84). Later in the conversation she characterizes someone as "pro-American" and is corrected by her boss: "*prodemocratic.*" Marie finds these concepts to be increasingly incompatible. Carol Gilligan writes (like Wilkinson, in 2018) that in electing Trump, the US experienced a "displacement of a democratic by a patriarchal framework" (Gilligan & Richards 2018: 6). Marie experiences this as well, explaining that the "men who'd been chosen to defend American interests abroad were so dysfunctional that it threw the whole undertaking into question ... There have been a lot of men in this world who have tried to shape it by getting it to conform to their own ideology" (Wilkinson 2018: 287–88).

Marie's discomfort in what she learns about American justice is underscored by a jarring second-person narration. The novel is told in the form of a letter she is writing to her young twin sons after an assassin broke into their Connecticut home and tried to kill them. She will finish the letter, a form halfway down the road of rumination, and then leave her sons with her mother in Martinique (they are "safer outside the US") so she can hunt down the man who gave the order. The choice of a second-person perspective means that Marie's story has neither first person's close identification with the individual sleuth, like in Paretsky or Cha, nor third person's locating of the sleuth in a community, like in Mina, Neely, or Head. So while the letter is to her sons, it also feels addressed to the reader. As a result, it asks the reader to consider how we hold ourselves accountable to the stories, both familial and national, that shape us.[36] The stories are messy. Perhaps unsurprisingly for a spy, Marie's favorite book is Nella Larsen's *Passing*. Marie reads it believing it will teach her something about her mysterious mother, who was "strong-armed … into passing for white" (Wilkinson 2018: 25) when she was sent from Martinique to New York City. Marie characterizes passing as both trauma and training. "I think the damage done to her," she writes, "by being forced to pass couldn't be undone, and she eventually came to feel like the only place she could truly be herself was here in Martinique" (Wilkinson 2018: 30). Initially, however, "she moved in and out of the New York places where Negroes were *interdits*, gathering her intelligence on the world that white people inhabited, always feeling like she was about to be made" (Wilkinson 2018: 26). Passing here is less signaling crime, as in Hopkins or Neely, than a kind of adaptation, a survival strategy for the socially vulnerable. She tells her boys "there's no better cover than one that depends on someone else's prejudices" (Wilkinson 2018: 162). Wilkinson suggests that Black fiction has always been part spy novel; her epigraph is taken from Ralph Ellison's *Invisible Man*: "son, after I'm gone I want you to keep up the good fight. I never told you, but our life is a war and I have been a traitor all my born days, a spy in the enemy's country ever since I give up my gun back in the Reconstruction." As with the Furies, the condition of being accepted into the democratic community – conditions set by those in power – is to renounce anger and the violence to which it can lead.

But Marie does not give up her gun. Her journey in and out of the FBI/CIA is fueled by anger. She is often "surprised by how angry" she is (Wilkinson 2018: 248). However, she is the poster child for regulated anger – for anger, as Lorde says, "focused with precision." It is a lesson she learns from her sister Helene, who teaches her how to box. In a match with Marie, Helene goes too far and "for an instant I saw that wild, girlhood fury of hers before she regained control of herself and backed away" (Wilkinson 2018: 78). Marie's sister remains a mystery for both Marie and the reader. The more we learn about her as Marie follows in her intelligence-work footsteps, the less we know. This is on purpose. Marie admits, as "much as I loved her, she could be a little duplicitous" (Wilkinson 2018: 26). Sisterhood is both essential to justice – figuring out who and what Helen was attached to and why she died is an important aspect of the novel – and elusive. Marie is more comfortable being a mother to her two sons than either a sister or a daughter.

---

[36] Claudia Rankine's multimodal work of poetry, *Citizen* (2014), also uses the second person to a similar effect, raising questions around anger, justice, and identity, albeit in a very different literary form.

Near the end of the novel she tells her boys that, upon learning of the death of their father, "had anyone who knows me been there to witness the intensity of my sorrow, they would've thought I'd lost my mind" (Wilkinson 2018: 267). But they should not mistake anger for madness. Marie explains that "You've likely never seen me like that. Almost no one has … The only anger I ever expose to the world is through implication, by suggesting that I'm on the brink of no longer being able to contain my fury. That is what a woman's strength looks like when it's palatable: like she is containing herself" (Wilkinson 2018: 267). Marie quietly seethes, but she also goes rogue, willing to kill when necessary. She herself does not believe in moral absolutes, writing to her sons "If what I'm telling you of our story means to you that the people it involves are either saved or damned, then you'll have misunderstood me" (Wilkinson 2018: 52). This is not the language of Nussbaum's clarity, nor Hopkins's or Neely's courtrooms, not of guilt nor innocence; this is the language of someone for whom a just outcome is indistinguishable from payback. The framing device of a letter to her sons, whom she is both fiercely protective of and also abandoning in her quest for vengeance, is a kind of perverted care. Can care be a solution for feminist crime fiction if the way to provide it is to take out the assassin threatening your loved ones? She concludes by telling her boys to resist injustice and that she hopes they'll "be good Americans" (Wilkinson 2018: 289). Knowing what she knows about "America," it is an odd conclusion – a bit like hovering around Jewel's grave, watching Blanche catch a bus, or Song pull up the grass. It holds us in that space of waiting, the indeterminate space of the spy. It is anger biding its time. What happens to its connections to justice when it snaps? The next section explores that question.

4 Losing It

This section acknowledges that female-centered crime narratives in the twenty-first century are becoming unmoored from narratives of justice. The women in these texts lose faith both in justice as the plot of crime narratives and in self-control as the way to achieve it. This is embodied in the rape-revenge story. Whereas rape was a feature of many of the texts in the previous section, and whereas closure was sometimes muted, as in Blanche's ruminations about her rapist's death, the mood of these works is more despairing. Anger here is not productive, but rather backwards-looking and self-destructive. These texts seem exhausted, not only with the structural violence of life under white capitalist hetero-patriarchy (as were the texts in the previous section), but also with calls for regulation or management of these ugly feelings. As Bogutskaya notes, being told to calm down often "makes you even less calm" (Bogutskaya 2023: 146).

These texts also understand, as Sara Ahmed explains, "how resilience becomes a deeply conservative technique" (Ahmed 2017: 189). Seen in this light, long-running detective series manifest the insanity of trying the same thing over and over and expecting a different outcome. These works reveal a skepticism about anger's capacity to alter the power relations that create injustice. Benedict S. Robinson has written recently that "perhaps anger is always more likely to reinforce than to overturn existing forms of power," and that "the terrible paradox of anger and empowerment may be that anger most empowers those who already have power" (Robinson 2023).

If care for loved ones and community is a way in which female sleuths have shown their commitment to justice since Anne Rodway nursed Mary Mallinson, the works in this section more often contain pathological care relationships. An early glimpse of this turn in the genre was the brutal rape of Lisbeth Salander by her "guardian" in *The Girl with the Dragon Tattoo*, one of the novels that surely marks the beginning of the blurry line between using it and losing it. In the works in this section, familial responsibilities (where they exist at all) are not simply hard to juggle, but are dysregulating. Attachments themselves turn violent in the lives of these unstable characters. Often told by unreliable or damaged narrators, this section also returns to crime fiction as a long-standing site for competing ideas of sanity and insanity.

Michaela Bronstein has written about "utopian crime," which is crime, almost always violent, "on behalf of a better future" (Bronstein 2017: 59). She looks at works, including the hard-boiled detective novel, that examine "gaps between law and morality" but which also cross "an ethical boundary," using violence where the outcome – a better future – is not guaranteed and "potentially monstrous" (Bronstein 2017: 59). The anger in the texts considered here often burns down the house, as Lady Audley did more than 150 years ago. Out of such smoldering embers might come, pace Bronstein, the start of something new. But it is a gamble. How can feminist texts balance a commitment to justice and care while being profoundly, and often entertainingly, violent at the same time? These texts don't know; characters here are often sleuths and killers at the same time. Today's female-centered crime narratives, when not cruelly optimistic, can't find the floor, like Beth in Megan Abbott's *Dare Me*, potentially tumbling to a violent end. This unstable balance is reflected in ugly feelings, but also in uncertain tones. Many of the texts in this section could be classified as both horror and comedy as well as crime fiction.[37] Today's crime fiction is side-stepping the earnest clarity of using anger in the fight for justice. Susan Sontag considers "camp" a mode that

---

[37] Hagelin and Silverman's *The New Female Antihero* (2022) covers both comedies as well as dramas. I am currently working on a project about "fugitive tone" in female crime fiction.

emerges when "sincerity is not enough" (Sontag 2001: 288). The tonal shifts in these uncertain works bear out an exhaustion with the pursuit of justice; these novels "aren't much for tidy endings" (Abbott 2018: 283).

4.1 Domestic Noir

Much of the discussion around this enormously successful subgenre is about its suspect feminism.[38] Do they portray (and potentially call out) a self-annihilating complicity with patriarchy, or do they feed into and profit from it? I come neither to bury nor to praise domestic noir, but to ask instead where is female anger in these popular texts? What do they add to our understanding that anger must be productive to serve justice? Anger manifests here in characters who are unlikeable, bored, entitled, violent, funny, manipulative, and, at times, however fleetingly, sympathetic. But justice is elusive, or sidelined altogether in favor of exploring the darkness, a place beyond safety. Noir is not interested in justice.[39] Discussing Gillian Flynn, Paretsky says the author of *Gone Girl* likes "being in the place where everything was unsafe." Paretsky finds this "terrifying. Gillian is a lovely person by the way, but I don't want to be in her head" (quoted in Cline 2022: 86). In domestic noir, there is no Captain Mallory helping Vic or Lieutenant Vanessa Sanchez helping Song. The police, even when they appear in these novels, seem irrelevant. Given the near-total whiteness of this subgenre, the police don't signal ideas about structural injustice that they might in crime novels by writers of color.[40] It is hard to locate female-centered crime narrative's characteristic connection to a broader social critique or to the power of community in these works. Anger is more likely to be isolating and self-destructive; it looks more like boredom than like fury, like an individualism unaware that, to paraphrase the words of indigenous activist Lilla Watson, our liberation is bound up with one another. The cultivation of one's self as an agentic individual is, of course, part of a traditional feminist narrative. But individuals in domestic noir are unstable: the payoff in this subgenre is the famous "twist," which tends to take the reader deeper into the

---

[38] Jacqueline Rose (2015) finds the "Girl" books (*Gone Girl*, *The Girl on the Train*) wanting. In her "Corkscrew in the Neck," she writes that "the giveaway is in the titles, their sly complicity with the diminishment of one half of the human race and a world that still permits it." But Leigh Redhead sees it differently: "After years of arse-kicking feminist detectives and plucky teenage action heroes, it seems that female characters are finally allowed to be morally complex" (Redhead 2018: 115). Robin Wasserman advocates for waiting to decide on whether the term is "plainly derogatory," as those labeled "girls" might still be "walking question marks" (Wasserman 2016).

[39] Or not entirely. Denise Mina has written recently that "the central mechanism of noir fiction is to create a justice deficit that needs to be redressed." That it is not always redressed does not disqualify noir fiction as a "form to explore social injustice" (Mina 2023).

[40] The novels of Kellye Garrett, author of *Like A Sister* (2022) and the upcoming *Missing White Woman* (2024), disrupt the racial logic of domestic noir.

murk and make them doubt what they thought they knew. Domestic noir does, however, illustrate the damage done by women's attempts to regulate themselves and their lives in a patriarchy: nearly all the novels feature characters monitoring their weight, their homes, and their families, contemplating the management skills required to "have it all." As Leigh Redhead says about Addy, the main character of Abbott's *Dare Me*, she "chooses to observe the tenets of postfeminism and neoliberalism: performance, self-surveillance, personal transformation, self-discipline and individualism. And by doing so she becomes a sociopath" (Redhead 2018: 123). In domestic noir regulation does not lead to justice but to madness.

No work better demonstrates this than Gillian Flynn's enormously successful *Gone Girl* (2012), also made into a successful movie (2014), about a woman perfect on the outside and damaged on the inside, seeking a kind of bloody justice that makes sense increasingly only to her. While author Julia Crouch coined the term "domestic noir," *Gone Girl*'s success – ninety-one weeks on the *New York Times* bestseller list – created the subgenre.[41] The novel's main character, Amy Dunne, is a latter-day Lady Audley, a woman whose youthful blond beauty lands her a seemingly ideal marriage. However, trapped by both disappointment and patriarchal femininity, she takes matters into her own potentially mad hands. In many ways domestic noir is a second coming of 1860s sensation fiction, asking the same question: are these feminist yawps, or merely entertainment on the way to putting women back in their boxes (nineteenth-century European asylums replaced by Brooklyn brownstones and London townhouses)? Both, answers Henry Sutton, noting that Amy "is both supervillain and superhero" (Sutton 2018: 58). Certainly it is messy, as Eva Burke explains that Amy's "sociopathic rationale complicates straightforward interpretation of her actions" (Burke 2018: 79). Messy as it is, there is a clear feminist argument at the literal center of the book: the famous "Cool Girl" speech. Amy explains that a Cool Girl is someone who loves cheap beer, sex, and hot dogs while "maintaining a size 2," someone "not even pretending to be the woman they want to be" but rather "pretending to be the woman a man wants them to be." The Cool Girl ideal has conned women, Amy sharply observes, "across the nation" to "collude in our degradation!" (Flynn 2014: 223). Above all, "Cool Girls never get angry" (Flynn 2014: 222).[42]

---

[41] See Eva Burke and Clare Clarke's "Introduction" to the *Clues* special issue on Domestic Noir (2021). They explain that Crouch came up with the term when she was asked to come up with marketing language for her debut novel, *Cuckoo* (2011).

[42] In a further example of history repeating itself, the viral monologue of this summer is Gloria's (played by America Ferrera) "impossible to be a woman" speech in 2023's messily feminist hit movie, *Barbie*.

Amy is angry about a lot of things: how her child psychologist parents created her into a character (the "Amazing Amy" of successful storybooks); how they profited off her perfection until they fecklessly had to borrow the money back; and about the faithlessness of her husband, Nick, for whom she claims to have felt genuine love until economic hard times and a hot 23 year old exposed that he was just like any other man and their perfect coupledom an illusion. Amy is a sophisticated critic of female anger, understanding that part of the traditional story is that women need to regulate it. So "Diary Amy" frequently makes the point that her anger is authentic but controlled: "Of course I *was* angry. I had *been* angry. But now I'm not" (Flynn 2014: 25); "I know I am going to be angry – that quick inhale, the lips going tight, the shoulders up, the *I so don't want to be mad but I'm going to be* feeling" (Flynn 2014: 65); "I swallow a quick gust of anger" (Flynn 2014: 155). Revenge Amy, the one we meet after the twist reveals Diary Amy to have been a performance, also has "discipline in spades" (Flynn 2014: 247), but she focuses it with precision in order to take Nick down. Amy's plan contains significant collateral damage; she frames and murders an old boyfriend, Desi, to account for her disappearance once her plan changes. Amy's actions, however brilliantly readable, are incommensurate with any notion of feminist justice. The novel raises but does not answer questions about the link between anger and madness that seem as problematic as they did in the nineteenth century. The terra firma of the Cool Girl speech starts to get soggy in the blood.

Paula Hawkins's *The Girl on the Train* (2015), an enormously popular novel (also turned movie), features a sociopathic man, Tom, who manages to convince multiple women that their problems have only to do with their own neuroses. But we don't know this aspect of Tom until, virtually, the end of the novel. While there is a violent resolution, the story is much more an exploration of the messy feelings of three women whose self-worth relies on male validation. There is anger, but it lurks beneath angsty self-hate and shameful self-doubt. This is the genre of "ugly feelings." Justice is not the point of the narrative – the point belongs to the fatal corkscrew. The anger that Amy Dunne regulates to the point of psychopathy and inflicts on others is turned inward in Rachel, our main narrator. She is the "girl" on the train, traveling to work (continuing even after she gets fired in order to conceal her shame from her roommate), past her old home, now inhabited by her ex and his new wife, Anna, and their baby (one of the reasons for the divorce was their inability to conceive a child, for which she blames herself). Rachel's train also passes a neighbor's home, whose perfect life she turns into salt for her own wounds until the woman, Megan, goes missing. Whatever anger is not turned inward (such as Rachel's alcoholism) manifests instead as toxic competition between the three women, all occupying some murky and only partially understood role in Tom's life. Anna is a classic unlikeable character: the one Tom left Rachel for. We see her alternating between boredom at staying at home with her baby, Evie – "I'm well aware there is no job more important than that of raising a child, but the problem is that it isn't valued. Not in the sense that counts to me at the moment, which is financial" (Hawkins 2015: 232) – and growing anger at Rachel's continued involvement with Tom. Spotting her on the street, Anna is "shaking with fury, digging my nails into my palms. Evie's kicking her feet in the air, and I'm so bloody angry, I don't want to pick her up for fear I would crush her" (Hawkins 2015: 234). In the novel's final pages, she understands that Tom is about to kill Rachel, and describes that glimpse of her future as "a fantasy." It is only self-interest that shapes her actions: she understands that she and her daughter would never be safe because she knows and "he won't be able to trust me" (Hawkins 2015: 312).

Megan has some context provided for her ugly feelings (she has lost both a child and a meaningful job), but she is increasingly seen as someone whose boredom is becoming dangerous. She falls into an affair with Tom (doing to Anna what Anna did to Rachel). She seduces her shrink, at one point losing her temper and "plot[ting] revenge" because he initially resists her advances. She suspects she is going mad, suffocating in her marriage with Scott, a controlling husband and hardly the ideal partner Rachel imagines from the train window. "When I close my eyes," Megan writes, "my head is filled with images of past and future lives, the things I dreamed I wanted, the things I had and threw away. I can't get comfortable, because every way I turn I run into dead ends: the closed gallery, the houses on this road, the stifling attentions of the tedious Pilates women" (Hawkins 2015: 163). Part of Megan's burgeoning madness is understood as unresolved trauma about the death of her daughter, due, in part, to her choices, but also (echoes of Lady Audley's story here) due to the abandonment of her husband who had "just gone off and left me" with the baby in a freezing, isolated home (Hawkins 2015: 169). Megan is punished by the novel for her appetites. She is assaulted by her husband when she tells him of the affair. Pregnant with Tom's baby, she confronts him. When she reacts with violent anger at Tom's dismissal of her, he kills her. Megan's disappearance turns this into a mystery, which Rachel tries to solve.

Rachel is more self-destructive than angry. She has put on weight, feels unattractive in the eyes of men (that women see themselves through a male gaze is constant in these novels), and loses her job. But as she tries to come up with a list of reasons why Megan might have disappeared (which she writes down on the back of a liquor store receipt), Rachel's pursuit of the "truth" leads her haltingly out of her alcoholic fog, a faint echo of the "using it" anger-to-justice plot. But it is faint: one of Rachel's recurring shameful memories, partially responsible for the end of her marriage, is of swinging a golf club at Tom in a "raging fury" (Hawkins 2015: 230). Anger is not the clarifying force it is for our female sleuths in "Using It" – indeed, for Rachel, anger is trapped in the haze of false memory. She wasn't swinging the golf club in anger, it turns out, but ducking in fear. This recovered memory does not lead to action. She calls the cops then hangs up: "Detective Riley . . . won't believe me. I know she won't" (Hawkins 2015: 271).

But when cornered by a murderous Tom, she plunges a corkscrew into his neck. A dystopic sisterhood is glimpsed as she and Anna, "side by side, drenched in his blood . . . sat on the sofa" (Hawkins 2015: 318). Anna and Rachel don't give each other up to the police, but the idea of solidarity is invoked in order to be dismissed. "Just before she parted, she touched my arm. 'You take care of yourself, Rachel,' she said, and there was something about the way she said it that made it feel like a warning" (Hawkins 2015: 323). Both *Gone Girl* and *The Girl on the Train*, like many domestic noir novels, contain a critique of how economic precarity shapes these women's lives: the sudden plummet from upper-class New York to the empty Midwestern mall in *Gone Girl*, the impossibility of making it out of the track-side starter home for Rachel and Tom (and then Anna and Tom), Megan's failed gallery. But, as critics have noted, it is a sad, upper-middle-class, straight, white, thin world. The kinds of intersectionality required by Lordean justice or even Paretsky's Chicago are invisible.

Ugly feelings are triumphant in Megan Abbott's *Dare Me* (2012). All of the toxic regulation of female bodies and emotions seen in *Gone Girl* and *The Girl on the Train* are here, but with actual girls. The "adult" world containing a legal system feels far away, even where there is a corpse and a perp hauled off to jail. The value system is askew: there is sympathy for the murderer, and some understanding that the victim didn't even want to live. This world is all gray area, limned by a combustible boredom: "There's something dangerous about the boredom of teenage girls" (Abbott 2013: 5). This is a portrait of the structures of seething as a young woman; however, justice in *Dare Me* only means the rightful cheer captain taking her place at long last. The novel begins with the arrival of a new coach, Colette French, who disrupts the carefully established power balance of the cheerleading squad ruled by Beth, the captain, and Addy, her "badass lieutenant" (Abbott 2013: 16), whose relationship has been forged over the years through episodes of complex intimacy and school-yard revenge. Addy "is a fille fatale for the postfeminist age" (Redhead 2018: 118), who slowly realizes her ambition to overtake Beth, a process caught up in her infatuation with the new coach. Coach French demotes Beth, who plots revenge. These girls are too bored to express their anger (over squad demotion, stringent beauty standards, problems at home) in clarifying ways. Whereas righteous anger might gather behind Juniper Song's eyes, Addy feels "the knot of hot boredom lodged behind your eyes, so thick and grievous you want to bang your head into the wall" (Abbott 2013: 72). Beth's eyes are similarly "shot through with blood and boredom" (Abbott 2013: 43).

Coach could be a woman from other domestic noir novels: thin, pretty, with a darling young daughter, Caitlin. By age twenty-two, she "had to fill" a house given to her by her seemingly perfect husband who told her to do "Whatever you want" (Abbott 2013: 60). But the home increasingly becomes a place of "irritation and woe" (Abbott 2013: 77), as Addy watches Coach enter into an affair with Sarge Will, a military recruiter at the high school, and then neglect all of her children, from Caitlin to the squad. As in other domestic noir novels, we are provided a small bit of backstory: Coach clearly suffered from untreated postpartum depression. Abbott flirts with locating the affect of these women within anger at patriarchal femininity. At one point, Addy sees Beth, as she tightens the screws on Coach, and "for a second I almost see all the misery and rage, centuries of it, tumbling across her face" (Abbott 2013: 223). However, there is no mention of this inherited rage elsewhere in the novel, and the emotional economy of the book is attuned to an interior power struggle. There is no sense of the wider world (with the notable exception of Sarge Will's post-duty PTSD), perfect for teenagers, but also revealing a disconnect from broader narratives of justice. After seeing the corpse of Sarge Will, Addy gets into her car: "Were I thinking straight, were I feeling the world made any sense at all, I might be driving to the police station, calling 911. Were I that kind of person. Instead, I look at my cell. I need to text Beth back" (Abbott 2013: 142).

Domestic noir leans into a question posed by writers of color in the previous section: what if the cause of your anger is not patriarchy, but, rather, other women? But where these "using it" novels retain a sense that sisterhood can be a part of the solution even if it is also part of the problem, domestic noir – and *Dare Me* in particular – chooses a commitment to community as its metaphor ... and topples it. The ultimate goal of this cheerleading squad is the building of a pyramid, "breathing something to life. Together. Each of us a singular organ feeding the other organs, creating something larger" (Abbott 2013: 21). Glimpsed from afar, as Emily, an injured member of the squad, does, it is dangerous: "it's like you're trying to kill each other and yourself" (Abbott 2013: 234). And Beth does almost die as she plunges from the top of the pyramid during the big game. As Addy consolidates her power, she remembers cheer advice from a previous coach, distinctly contrary to the logic of the pyramid: *"Time comes, you have to listen to yourself"* (Abbott 2013: 213 [emphasis original]). And she does.

4.2 Assassins

Crime fiction has long featured female spies and assassins, part strong female sleuth and part femme fatale. From *La Femme Nikita* to *The Americans'* Elizabeth Jennings and *Homeland*'s Carrie Mathieson, these characters' behavior is complex, violent, and unlikeable.[43] It is also grounded in belief (about the CIA, Russia, national security) and while belief is not justice (and can be delusional), it is an attachment to an idea; anger is put in service of something. This section will look at works where that attachment, a distinction between good guys and bad guys, blurs into irrelevancy; as assassin Villanelle tells agent Eve in *Killing Eve*, "I think if you went high enough you'd probably find we work for the same people." Natsuo Kirino's *Out*, Gu Byeong-Mo's *The Old Woman with the Knife*, and the BBC series *Killing Eve* feature a range of ultraviolent women. Assassins share some of the problems faced by our earlier angry women. Professional killing is a kind of dystopic "using it" – where precision becomes psychopathy. Like the isolated women of domestic noir, assassins are nightmare individualists. Sisterhood is not a solution (neither is motherhood). As Hornclaw, the assassin in *The Old Woman with the Knife*, says, "No teamwork required" (Gu 2022: 110).

Out, published in Japan in 1997 but translated into English in 2003, shares some elements of a domestic noir novel. Four coworkers (given the toxicity of their interpersonal dynamics, it is not quite right to call them friends) work the nightshift in a boxed-lunch factory situated in a noirish Tokyo characterized by rapacious capitalism and organized crime. Their criminal career begins with one of the women snapping at home: a young wife and mother strangles her abusive and philandering husband after he asks her "can't you be nice once in a while?" (Kirino 2003: 48). She asks one of her coworkers to help dispose of the body, and the novel follows their exploits as they sink deeper and deeper into the blood. While the anxieties stemming from the 2008 financial crisis cast a pall over the characters in domestic noir novels, the rigged patriarchal economy of late twentieth-century Japan is a more tactile presence in *Out*. Kirino has been a critic of Japan's patriarchal capitalism and its deleterious effects on gender roles and society: "Men and women are not on good terms in Japanese society. They don't get along. There is too much gender-specific role division. Men are almost like slaves in the corporate world and Japanese women are contained within the household. That is one of the sources of this boiling rage" (quoted in Nakanishi 2018: 127). That might be the novel's

---

[43] Hagelin and Silverman's chapter on *Homeland* is a fascinating exploration of how imbricated narratives of madness and female anger remain central to the representation of women in popular culture (Hagelin & Silverman 2022: 95–114).

message, but its main concern is the ugly feelings of the four women. While the story is told in the third person, all these characters are given time in the novel to reveal their innermost thoughts. Kuniko, Yoshie, Yayoi, and Masako represent a range of female lives under patriarchy. Kuniko is self-hating, competitive, and materialistic, someone for whom "everything would be okay if she bought a new foundation" (Kirino 2003: 301). While no one deserves Kuniko's fate, by the time her corpse is delivered as both another job (they need to cut her up) and a warning to the other three, the novel dares the reader to care. Yoshie is a widow taking care of her abusive mother-in-law. Yoshie's only reason for living is because none of her dependents, including her demanding and disappointing children, "could get along without her" (Kirino 2003: 23), but that doesn't quell "an urge to strangle the old bitch" (Kirino 2003: 25). Yayoi, "the best looking of the four woman," is the flawless young beauty of domestic noir, complete with "cluttered and volatile feelings" (Kirino 2003: 7) and the jealousy of other women: "her looks were so conspicuous at the factory that a number of women had taken to bullying her" (Kirino 2003: 6). And then there is Masako, whose professional career was limited by sexism, and who has taken the night shift at the boxed-lunch factory for only partially understandable reasons, one of which is to flee an unfulfilling home life with her husband and son: "the three of them were so completely estranged that it was hard to understand why they lived together" (Kirino 2003: 72).

At first, we assume that the relationships between these women, even amidst the bleak realities of their life on the assembly line, will provide the logic of the novel. But ultimately, like *Dare Me*'s cheer squad, it leads them all into further horror. A detective speculating about who helped get rid of the body of Yayoi's murdered husband concludes "in this case there ... didn't seem to be much basis for the 'sisterhood' idea that tended to drive these things" (Kirino 2003: 209). After Yayoi kills her husband, taking a minute to enjoy it – "strange that she'd never known she had such cruelty inside; still, she found this thrilling" (Kirino 2003: 48) – she calls Masako, who is immediately "willing to help." Kirino does not provide a reason. Masako comes up with the idea of cutting the body up into disposable pieces. This takes place in her bathroom and, if you could overlook that they are dismembering the father of Yayoi's children, the detailed description of blood and grouting ("it might cause problems if bits of flesh got stuck between the tiles" Kirino 2003: 74) might read as dark comedic commentary on domestic labor. Masako enlists the help of the other women through a combination of guilt, manipulation, and money. As in *Gone Girl*, the official justice system plays a role, detectives lurk around and ask questions, but it seems invoked in order to be dismissed as outside the concerns of this novel.

What are the concerns of the novel? There is plenty of crime and examination of its meaning, but few conclusions. Yayoi's killing of her husband could be read as revenge, but this happens so early in the novel that it seems like a precondition rather than a verdict. There is a potential rapist haunting the factory parking lot, who turns out to be an itinerant worker from Brazil. He attempts to assault Masako, who initially "felt a surge of dark rage," but ultimately befriends him because of the "sense of the isolation they shared" (Kirino 2003: 225). The women are drawn into the dismembering business both because they need money for pedestrian things like school field trips and foundation, and also because they find themselves in a cat-and-mouse game with a real villain who they temporarily lead the police to believe is responsible. This villain, Satake, is a psychopath who has recently returned to his life of organized crime after serving prison time for raping and murdering a woman, a repulsive sexual obsession (no justice-adjacent rumination here) that he will transfer onto Masako. The novel blurs the lines between Satake and Masako (as it does between Bullfight and Hornclaw in *The Old Woman and the Knife* and Eve and Villanelle in *Killing Eve*): "Was she the hunter or the hunted? Would she kill or be killed? . . . She and Satake were at war" (Kirino 2003: 362). The idea of justice collapses if the two sides are indistinguishable. If Masako initially worries that her ability to chop up bodies "was possibly the sign of a sick mind, there was a part of her that was exhilarated by the challenge" (Kirino 2003: 70). Masako's murky motivations remain the primary mystery of this novel.

There is a brief glimpse that anger might be a motivation: "Anger – that was what she felt. She had no idea who or what she was angry at, but at least she'd put a name to her emotion . . . Now she realized that the anger had been liberating" (Kirino 2003: 225). But there's a lot of novel left, and the vibe is more numb than angry. "If you could numb yourself to all the blood and gore," Kirino writes, "there was really very little difference between this job and the one they did at the factory" (Kirino 2003: 283). But numbing yourself to the blood and gore is a big ask for readers: the showdown between Satake and Masako is almost unreadably sadistic. If this is feminist crime fiction, whither feminism? As if to toy with the feminist idea about the clarifying effects of anger, in the middle of the battle-to-the-death with Satake, Masako has "rage in her voice, but her words were slurred now from the beating" (Kirino 2003: 387). It also toys with all the characters' proximity to madness. Masako finds it "almost inevitable that so many of the women who worked [the night shift] should end up slightly crazy" (Kirino 2003: 292). Yoshie, channeling Lady Audley, sets a fire, killing her mother-in-law, as "a way out after all" (Kirino 2003: 378) and bikes off into the night. It also toys with a potential happy ending, the "out" hinted at in the novel's title. Masako's stalker-friend invites her to visit him in Brazil and gives her his address on a slip of paper.

This idea literally goes down the drain (Masako tears it up and drops it down a culvert). Masako ends the novel regretting her murder of Satake, not because she is haunted by the killing (no ruminating on accountability here) but because she misses him; she wanted him to survive "because I understand you now" (Kirino 2003: 398). But we never understand Masako. She finds herself, a perpetrator and a survivor, alone in the end. The novel has a circular rhythm: it begins with her wondering "where did she want to go? She felt lost" (Kirino 2003: 3); it concludes with her waiting for an elevator, which "moaned like the wind" (Kirino 2003: 400).

Gu Byeong-Mo's international bestseller *The Old Woman with the Knife* was first written in the moment of domestic noir (2013), but it was not translated into English until recently (2022). It asks some of the same questions about the slow violence of neoliberalism that our other texts have, and it provides a significant amount of gore with some graphic fight scenes, but overall the feelings are less ugly than in *Out*, perhaps befitting a novel organized around the thoughts of a senior citizen. It is, nevertheless, not about justice. Our "hero" is Hornclaw, a highly skilled assassin who, at sixty-five, is approaching the end of her career. Her nickname, given to her by the head of the "disease control" agency where she works, blurs lines, too. Hornclaw "signified aggression, but an animal's horns and claws were protective as well" (Gu 2022: 45). She keeps her nails short, however, to "conceal the aggression inherent in the owner of the fingernails" (Gu 2022: 45). Hornclaw is all about concealing her feelings, following the advice of Ryu, her mentor and, later, companion: "*You can't last in this line of work if you show your feelings. It doesn't matter if it's rage or discomfort or regret. . . . And you're a woman, which means you'll often have to ignore insults*" (Gu 2022: 44 [original emphasis]). By the time we meet her, she has long been detached from her feelings; anger is a kind of strategy: "she gathers rage to fill the emptiness. She holds on to that feeling so that her anger doesn't sour into fear" (Gu 2022: 232). Her relationship with her rescue dog, Deadweight, is the emotional center of the novel but also a study in the meeting of minimal needs. The dog "politely wags her tail" when Hornclaw returns home, offering up "a concise, dry greeting, perhaps what she perceives to be the minimum requirement of a cohabitant" (Gu 2022: 114–115). Her thoughts about care for the animal are darkly humorous: she creates a window for Deadweight to get out if she doesn't return from a job, or if she dies of old age at home. She wouldn't mind if Deadweight ate her "if that helps you for a bit," but people will "think that a dog who ate its owner's corpse isn't in its right mind and can't live a normal life" (Gu 2022: 117). The reader doesn't know whether to laugh or to cry.

Hornclaw's backstory, like for so many of these characters, is painful and provides a partial explanation for her difficulty with emotions. She is one of several children, and is critical of parents who couldn't provide and yet still were like pigs "mating, oinking and having litter after litter" (Gu 2022: 122). Hornclaw's criticisms implicate patriarchy (her parents were "old-fashioned ignoramuses [who] kept having baby after baby until they finally had a boy"; Gu 2022: 122), as well as a class system that has poorer relations serve their wealthier relatives. She works for her cousins as a servant, and, in a moment of weakness, tries on and hides her cousin's jewelry. When they suspect she is a thief, she "spiraled with rage, forgetting that she had caused them to mistrust her" (Gu 2022: 127); her instinctive violent response sends a cousin to the hospital. She is taken under the wing of an assassin, who uses her as a lure. When the client makes an aggressive sexual advance on her, she reveals her talent at murder. Her feelings are murky – like "rice-washed water" (Gu 2022: 161). Her closest tie is to Ryu, who took her in, was the father of a baby given up for adoption, but also turned her into an assassin. When she tries to explain her feelings to him, she "mashed all of her feelings together and euphemistically called it a burden" (Gu 2022: 189).

The affective wires of our female assassins are crossed. Hornclaw describes her work using a metaphor both maternal and murderous: "she feels connected to the work as if by an umbilical cord. An umbilical cord that manages barely to provide just enough nutrition before suddenly wrapping itself around your neck, choking you to death" (Gu 2022: 81). As the image suggests, this book is not sentimental about traditional family ties. At the heart of the story is a boy who witnessed the traumatic aftermath of his father's murder – by Hornclaw, posing as a temporary nanny. The boy's mother moves on after the murder and the boy, abandoned, becomes Bullfight, the young assassin at Hornclaw's agency and her clear nemesis. But even he is not enacting a clear revenge: "He never daydreamed of acting out the plot of some third-rate martial arts novel, of finding the woman who bashed in his father's head and exacting revenge ... Most of what happened was a collage, created by the shapes and layers of unimportant events. His life was a totality of somehows" (Gu 2022: 108–109). Much like Satake, Bullfight is all violent instincts with no clear outlet (patriarchy has done them no favors either). Bullfight never learns who ordered his father's killing and so fixates on Hornclaw. The novel, like *Out*, (nearly) concludes with their final showdown.

Gu is not Paretsky nor even Kirino, but there is a social critique here of a Korean society where recession lurks, when Hornclaw thinks about setting up a small fried-chicken-and-beer joint to support her retirement. She thinks it could work "as long as she doesn't expand the business too fast or become the victim of gentrification or get swindled and lose everything" (Gu 2022: 31). Korean society is becoming less respectful of its economically vulnerable elders

: "the only time anyone pays attention to senior citizens on the subway is when they bump into people as they carry a bundle of discarded newspapers scavenged from one end of the train to the other" (Gu 2022: 12). Small business owners are bullied by larger corporations that make use of professional killers. Such a practice is on the rise: Hornclaw observes that "more and more specialists are entering the profession" (Gu 2022: 104). There is also a subtle feminist critique on how aging is particularly challenging for women. But this novel is disinterested in justice. Hornclaw does not see what she does as justice, trained by Ryu, who explained it this way: *"I won't say I do it because someone has to. It's laughable to say it's for justice. But if the money I make by getting rid of vermin can be used later, that doesn't seem to be a bad thing, does it?"* (Gu 2022: 33 [original emphasis]). She has a faint moral compass – she attempts to spare people from unnecessarily painful deaths – but doesn't overly explore what she does: all "she knows is how to kill, not how to save someone" (Gu 2022: 256). So she is surprised by her actions at the end, where she attempts to save a child, the daughter of a doctor who saves her life at the beginning of the novel. Bullfight has kidnapped the child as bait (as Hornclaw once was) in order to provoke a showdown. The ending of the novel offers up the possibility of a range of "just" outcomes – the rescue of the child, the defeat of Bullfight – even, perhaps, Bullfight's defeat of Hornclaw (revenge for the murder of his father).

But Bullfight isn't sure what he wants and he dies uncertain whether Hornclaw even recognized that he was that little boy who found his father's murdered body (she did). The kidnapped girl cleverly manages to call for help, but the operator doubts her report, "having a hard time believing what the child is reporting and asks the same questions over and over again" (Gu 2022: 261). There is an explosion, and so the police are expected, but they never arrive. We never see the reunion of the family or any kind of gratitude toward Hornclaw for saving the child's life. Instead of closure, we get a vivid description of Bullfight and Hornclaw's final battle, which has the detail and affective murkiness of *Out*'s ultraviolent denouement. There are knives and guns, hands are shot off, weapons wedged in muscles, and faces sliced. Hornclaw "stabs him in the lower abdomen and drags her knife up near his liver, causing Bullfight to topple over onto her. A bystander might think they are lovers embracing, not in the throes of a grisly fight" (Gu 2022: 63). In the final pages, Gu pivots to an equally detailed description of the manicure business, nearly as competitive as that of disease control specialists, where the now one-armed Hornclaw makes a first visit. She gets her nails (all five of them – is this a joke?) done with an elaborate pattern that evokes "fireworks in the night sky" (Gu 2022: 278). If short nails concealed her aggression, these longer nails are an open signifier: hopeful? a different kind of disguise? As a kind-of-happy ending, it registers the same false note that *Lady Audley's Secret* does. You can almost hear Gu saying, a la Braddon, "I hope no one will take objection to my story because the end of it" trades the "broken, bruised, warped nails" of an assassin for one "bright shining moment" before she crumbles "like overripe fruit" (Gu 2022: 279–80).

This inscrutable tone brings us back to where we began and the phenomenological bog of the genre-breaking assassin show, *Killing Eve*, based on the novellas by Luke Jennings. In her *Good and Mad*, Rebecca Traister notes that women "regularly ingest cultural messages that suggest that women's rage is irrational, dangerous, or laughable" (Traister 2018: xxvi). *Killing Eve*, with its crazy, murderous, and hilarious characters, delivers. Each of the central three characters, Villanelle (Jodie Comer), Eve Polastri (Sandra Oh), and Carolyn Martens (Fiona Shaw), raise most of the issues considered in this *Element*. Villanelle is a latter-day Lady Audley, who looks like a domestic noir damsel (or, as Margaret Oliphant said of Lady Audley, a "fair-haired demon"), but is putting it to use as an assassin. Eve, with her rumpled overcoat and poor eating habits, is a classic sleuth figure, working for both MI5 and MI6 in the course of the series. But both are more complicated. Eve is getting in touch with a slowly simmering antisociality that gives her a fascination with and insight into female psychopathy. And they are bored: Eve with her perfectly nice marriage to Nico, and Villanelle, who turns boredom (and murder) into a fine art. Boredom, a state in which "the self has difficulty accessing authenticity, productivity, and desire," reflects the directionless nature of this show (Pease 2012: vii). These women are uncertain about what they want, other than each other in a vague and deferred way. The show is both incredibly stylish and bloody (there are multiple online sites ranking the gruesomeness of Villanelle's kills). If Eve and Villanelle are ensnared in a messy cat-and-mouse game, master spy Carolyn Martens is the portrait (or caricature?) of female regulation, from her laser sharp hairstyle and wardrobe, to the (slight) glimpse we get of her anguish over her son Kenny's murder. After dismissing the explicit, needy grief of her daughter, Carolyn retires to her bedroom, lies down, and slowly clinches a pillow over her face. Are these women angry? Bored? Psychopaths? Yes. Are we supposed to find this funny? Horrifying? Stylish? Yes. But for fans of the crime narrative genre, trained to take a side, it is hard to know what to root for. Is the humor just one more way to obscure female anger? Both critics and fans were much more critical of the final two seasons, and one has to wonder if that's because the first seasons' clever flaunting of the conventions of crime fiction created its own dead end. What would justice, or even closure, look like for this messy series?

It is possible to read *Killing Eve* not only as a return of the repressed Lady Audley, but also of Nussbaum's Furies: it is no coincidence that there are three main characters in *Killing Eve*. It is also no coincidence that we are killing "Eve," the first female detective who found Eden boring and sought the power to know.[44] The first season initiates but does not see through a clarifying revenge plot for the murder of Eve's beloved boss, Bill; the final season ends with Eve gouging out a woman's eyes with her bare hands and she and Villanelle working to take down "The Twelve," Villanelle's original employer.

The trajectory of Carolyn does not provide any clarity: she is both in charge of tracking down "The Twelve," and, as we learn in the final season, a founding member. If justice depends on focusing our anger with precision, we are out of luck. Villanelle's "madness" is treated like a condition but is also rooted in childhood trauma and professional grooming. The show offers up both nature and nurture ... and shrugs, to an amazing soundtrack. The final season continues to toy with us, speaking to a desire for Villanelle's redemption by having her find God (also played by Jodie Comer in a campy mustache). She slaughters members of the congregation. Eve and Carolyn both pursue Villanelle as she moves in and out of prisons throughout the series, playing with the idea of containment, of our quest for a kind of regulation of chaos, of our expectations for a justice system to manage crime. To paraphrase Nussbaum, you don't put Villanelle in a cage and come out with justice.

So what are we watching for? If you watch *Killing Eve* as a love story, you are rooting for the union of one psychopath and one psychopathy-adjacent character, and you are ultimately punished for this desire by having Villanelle killed just as this possibility is coming into view, sinking into the ooze of the Thames. If you watch it for some kind of justice (for the world? please, but at least for Bill and Kenny, two characters whose deaths stand out amidst the dozens as sincerely heart-wrenching), that is incompatible with the love story resolution you were just hoping for. Is this show, like so many of the female-centered ultraviolent stories in crime fiction right now, just done? *Killing Eve* seems to recognize our need for a narrative something. The final season charts the grooming of a new assassin, Pam, a bullied mortician who kills her abusive brother in a highly regulated rage only to find herself in the path of The Twelve. And Carolyn. In a scene signaling another key moment of female madness, Pam and Carolyn forge an understanding by floating fully clothed in a lake, evoking the image of Waterhouse's Ophelia. Pam is becoming part of the crew, interacting also with both Eve and Villanelle. Ultimately, however, Pam walks away. She refuses the futures these women offer. We don't know where she goes, but she goes. This nonending amidst the narrative wreckage is both pleasing and uncomfortable, because to root

---

[44] Maria Tatar's *The Heroine with 1,001 Faces* (2021) discusses Eve and the punishment of female curiosity and transgressive behavior.

for Pam to make her way to a less toxic place is to ignore the other lessons of the show, to engage in cruel optimism's "attachment to dreams we know are destined to be dashed" (Hsu 2019). I have always wanted female-centered crime fiction to be a place where female anger can lead to justice, but it feels naïve wanting stories of justice in a world where, at least in the US, guns have more rights than women. Bring on the Furies.

Or maybe just Michaela Coel.

5 Epilogue

Coel's critically acclaimed miniseries *I May Destroy You* doesn't answer all of the questions raised by this Element, but it does take anger, intersectional feminism, and justice seriously, and it doesn't sink itself in the Thames. A twelve-part series that debuted in 2020, *I May Destroy You* tells the story of Arabella ("Bella," played by Coel), a promising author (her first novel, *Chronicles of a Fed-up Millennial*, was published on Twitter) who is struggling with her second book and running out of time on her publisher's deadline. When she takes a writing break to meet some friends, she is drugged and raped in the bar's bathroom stall. As she tries to investigate what happened to her, and struggles to cope, we see the violent assault ripple throughout the lives of her friends, such as besties Terry and Kwame, and an old friend Simon, who invited her to the bar in the first place. Bella's hazy memories threaten her sanity and career. As she is trying to get her life back together, in support groups and on social media, she has another experience with sexual assault when Zain, a consensual partner, removes a condom without her consent. The original title of the series was *January 22*, the date of Coel's own rape while she worked on her previous show, *Chewing Gum*. The deeply personal and complex story reflects the process of someone reflecting in real time on what her options are for finding justice, while also dealing with her anger and trauma. In keeping with the pitchy tone of these contemporary works, *I May Destroy You* is described as a comedy-drama. It *is* both funny and harrowing, and as stylish in its own way as *Killing Eve*.

Though *I May Destroy You* is a very different show to *Killing Eve*, it, too, tries out a lot of the things that we associate with female-centered crime narrative. There is a violent assault, there are blurry lines: one of the most notable elements of the show is that everyone, when seen over the course of their lives, is, at times, both victim and perpetrator. There is a recourse to the police who are, in keeping with the pitchiness, both sympathetic (there is a Black female cop, Officer Funmi, who deals with Bella's case) and useless (the flustered homophobic panic of the white cops who field Kwame's report of assault). It treats each character as a potentially isolated individual, bearing secrets, while keeping them, sometimes harmfully and sometimes lovingly, interdependent on one another. It locates these individuals' lives in a structurally violent culture shaped by legacies of imperialism, racism, the impact of runaway social media, homophobia, classism, and sexism. It also locates them in communities of care. It also engages with the idea that Bella is a bit mad, as her mind works to recover her memory and also plays tricks on her. Coel's incredibly expressive face shifts from anger, to fear, to confusion, to a mask; it is often hard to know which emotion she is feeling.

The final episode of *I May Destroy You* both directs and misdirects our anger. There are multiple endings, featuring various of the paths explored by our justice-seeking characters in this Element: taking revenge, breaking down, reversing roles, moving on. The viewer doesn't grasp this at first and so fully inhabits them, experiencing, fleetingly, the closure that each path affords. E. Alex Jung remarks that "the beauty of the ending is in how it contains shards of reality, but expands them into strange, surprising shapes, like blowing hot glass" (Jung 2020). Hot glass indeed: these endings spin and shape the shapeless rage of women into a simultaneous desire for and despair of justice. Coel, in an interview, recalls having justice in the forefront of her mind as she was writing the show, thinking "here's a way no one has to die but there's still justice" (Jung 2020). None of the endings are unjust, but none of them are perfectly just. In one ending, *I May Destroy You* inhabits the rape-revenge story that it could be. Bella spots her attacker, David, at the bar and plots revenge with the help of Terry and Theodora, a childhood frenemy whose own earlier allegations of sexual assault are tinged with racism and classism, and whose survivors' support group Bella joins. The women beat him to death on the streets of London and Bella returns to her apartment, stashing his bloody corpse under her bed. We only realize this is a fantasy when the scene repeats: we stare again into Coel's eyes, as her far-off look takes us back to the bar, where she encounters David in the bathroom stall. This time he has a breakdown, and our focus is on his damage, rather than Bella's. Hurt people hurt people. A third version has them in a romantic relationship, where she penetrates him, assuming the position Zain occupied in his assault of her. Finally, we see her staying in her apartment, surrounded by her chosen family, who have all been part of both her trauma and her healing. She has finally finished the book she struggled to write. Through the multiple endings, and our watching of each one as the "real" one, this show enacts Bella's anger and its search for justice as waiting, time taken to mourn selves who have been lost, to grieve a community connected by harm as much as by love. In none of the endings, however, is Bella represented as crazy. There is no Belgian madhouse awaiting her, but rather an independent book store full of readers and friends celebrating the publication of her book.

The multiple endings and the modal verb "may" in the title capture the structures of seething. Coel takes us on a journey through Bella's anger, which is simultaneously lurking behind her eyes, beneath a stylish surface, or, literally, embodied as a bloody corpse underneath her bed. Bella's "I may destroy" retains the possibility of destruction (she is biding her time, yes, she has the capacity to act), and the "I" gives her first-person agency, but the "may" pauses the action, enabling rumination on accountability. There is violence and the threat of violence, but there is clear feminist interest in how to care for one's self and others – even if they have caused harm. Sisterhood is not perfect, but it is forgiven. Coel's multiple timelines and Bella's emphasis on messy community undercut any sense of individualistic resilience. The "you" of the title makes the relationship between victim and villain both clear and not clear: it depends on who's talking. The multiple endings of *I May Destroy You* reflect the many different kinds of contemporary stories about female anger in popular culture today: of graphic violence but also of care, of individual isolation and collectivity, of waiting to know what to do with what we know.

Female-centered crime narratives are largely skeptical of and increasingly disinterested in official justice, in ways that are both threatening and liberating. Structures of seething require a modal verb; it holds us on the reflective cusp of action, but centers process instead of payback or precision. As Brittney Cooper admits: "my anger and rage haven't always been 'focused with precision.' The process, of both becoming a feminist and becoming okay with rage as a potential feminist superpower, has been messy as hell. We need to embrace our messiness more. We need to embrace the ways we are in process more" (Cooper 2018: 5–6). Angry women may destroy you, or they may mourn the victims of destruction (including themselves). As Blanche says, we "all played a part in this mess, but we ain't all equally responsible" (Neely 2000: 315). Is this justice? It may be.

References

Abbott, M. (2013). *Dare Me*. Back Bay Books.
Abbott, M. (2018). Afterword: The Woman Through the Window. In *Domestic Noir: The New Face of 21st Century Crime Fiction*, ed. L. Joyce and H. Sutton. Palgrave Macmillan, pp. 281–284.
Ahmed, S. (2017). *Living a Feminist Life*. Duke University Press.
Anderson, A., Felski, R., and Moi, T. (2019). *Character: Three Inquiries in Literary Studies*. University of Chicago Press.
Bailey, M. (2021). *Misogynoir Transformed: Black Women's Digital Resistance*. New York University Press.
Berlant, L. (2008). *The Female Complaint*. Duke University Press.
Berlant, L. (2011). *Cruel Optimism*. Duke University Press.
Bogutskaya, A. (2023). *Unlikeable Female Characters: The Woman Pop Culture Wants You to Hate*. Sourcebooks.
Braddon, M. E. (1987). *Lady Audley's Secret*. Oxford University Press.
Bronstein, M. (2017). Four Generations, One Crime. In *Crime Fiction as World Literature*, ed. L. Nilsson, D. Damrosch, and T. D'haen. Bloomsbury, pp. 59–74.
Browder, L. (2006). Dystopian Romance: True Crime and the Female Reader. *The Journal of Popular Culture*, 39: 928–953.
Burke, E. (2018). From Cool Girl to Dead Girl: *Gone Girl* and the Allure of Female Victimhood. In *Domestic Noir: The New Face of 21st Century Crime Fiction*, ed. L. Joyce and H. Sutton. Palgrave Macmillan, pp. 71–86.
Burke, E. (2021). Interview with Julia Crouch. *Clues: A Journal of Detection* 39(1), 99–103.
Burke, E. and Clarke, C. (2021). Introduction: Domestic Noir. *Clues: A Journal of Detection* 39(1), 5–11.
Butler, J. (2004). *Precarious Life: The Powers of Mourning and Violence*. Verso.
Cha, S. (2013). *Follow Her Home*. Minotaur Books.
Cha, S. (2014). *Beware* Beware. Minotaur Books.
Cha, S. (2015). *Dead Soon Enough*. Minotaur Books.
Chandler, R. (1992). *The Big Sleep*. Vintage.
Chemaly, S. (2018). *Rage Becomes Her: The Power of Women's Anger*. Atria.
Chen, T. (2005). *Double Agency: Acts of Impersonation in Asian American Literature and Culture*. Stanford University Press.

References

Cherry, M. (2018). The Errors and Limitations of Our "Anger-Evaluating" Ways. In *The Moral Psychology of Anger*, ed. M. Cherry and O. Flanagan. Rowman and Littlefield.

Cherry, M. (2021). *The Case for Rage*. Oxford University Press.

Clarke, C. (2020). *British Detective Fiction 1891–1901: The Successor to Sherlock Holmes*. Palgrave Macmillan.

Cline, S. (2022). *After Agatha: Women Write Crime*. Oldcastle Books.

Cole, C. (2004). *Private Dicks and Feisty Chicks: An Interrogation of Crime Fiction*. Curtin University Press.

Collins, W. (1856). The Diary of Anne Rodway. *Household Words* July 19, 26. www.djo.org.uk/household-words/volume-xiv/page-1.html.

Conan Doyle, A. (1977). The Adventure of the Copper Beeches. In *Adventures of Sherlock Holmes*. Ballantine, pp. 263–289.

Conan Doyle, A. (1994). Charles Augustus Milverton. In *The Return of Sherlock Holmes*. Oxford World's Classics, pp. 157–175.

Cooper, B. (2018). *Eloquent Rage: A Black Feminist Finds Her Superpower*. St. Martin's.

Crenshaw, K. (1991). Mapping the Margins: Intersectionality, Identity, and Violence Against Women of Color. *Stanford Law Review* 43(6), 1242–1300.

Cruz, L. (2015). The New True Crime. *Atlantic*. June 11.

Evans, L. (2021). The Girl Who Got Mad: Challenging Psychopathology in Domestic Noir's Antiheroine via Sarah Vaughn's *Anatomy of a Scandal*. *Clues* 39(1), 36–46.

Felski, R. (2015). *The Limits of Critique*. The University of Chicago Press.

Fisher, P. (2002). *The Vehement Passions*. Princeton University Press.

Flynn, G. (2014). *Gone Girl*. Broadway Books.

Forrester, A. (2012). *The Female Detective*. The British Library.

Geller, J. L. and Harris, M. (1994). *Women of the Asylum: Voices from Behind the Walls, 1840–1945*. Doubleday.

Gilbert, S. and Gubar, S. (1984). *The Madwoman in the Attic: The Woman Writer and the Nineteenth-Century Literary Imagination*. Yale University Press.

Gilbert, S. and Gubar, S. (2021). *Still Mad: American Women Writers and the Feminist Imagination*. Norton.

Gilligan, C. and Richards, D. A. J. (2018). *Darkness Now Visible: Patriarchy's Resurgence and Feminist Resistance*. Cambridge University Press.

Gilligan, C. and Snider, N. (2018). *Why Does Patriarchy Persist?* Polity Press.

Grafton, S. (1982). *"A" is for Alibi*. Henry Holt.

Green, A. K. (1997). An Intangible Clue. In *Twelve Women Detective Stories*, ed. L. Marcus. Oxford, pp. 147–166.

Green, A. K. (2013). *The Mysteries of Amelia Butterworth*. Palmera.

Gu, B.-M. (2022). *The Old Woman With the Knife*. Hanover Square Press.

Hagelin, S. and Silverman, G. (2022). *The New Female Antihero: The Disruptive Women of Twenty-First Century US Television*. Chicago University Press.

Hamilton, C. S. (2021). *Sara Paretsky: Detective Fiction as Trauma Literature*. Manchester University Press.

Hawkins, P. (2015). *The Girl on the Train*. Riverhead Books.

Hayward, W. S. (2013). *Revelations of a Lady Detective*. The British Library.

Head, C. A. (2016). *Bury Me When I'm Dead*. Bywater.

Head, C. A. (2018). *Wake Me When It's Over*. Bywater.

Hefner, B. E. (2021). *Black Pulp: Genre Fiction in the Shadow of Jim Crow*. Minnesota University Press.

hooks, b. (1995). *Killing Rage: Ending Racism*. Henry Holt.

Hopkins, P. E. (2021a). *Hagar's Daughter*. Broadview.

Hopkins, P. E. (2021b). Talma Gordon. In *Hagar's Daughter*. Broadview, pp. 303–318.

Hsu, H. (2019). Affect Theory and the New Age of Anxiety. *The New Yorker*. March 25. www.newyorker.com/magazine/2019/03/25/affect-theory-and-the-new-age-of-anxiety.

I May Destroy You. (2020). HBO/BBC.

Jagger, A. (1989). Love and Knowledge: Emotion in Feminist Epistemology. *Inquiry* 32(2), 151–176.

Joyce, L. and Sutton, H. (eds.) (2018). *Domestic Noir: The New Face of 21st Century Crime Fiction*, ed. L. Joyce and H. Sutton. Palgrave.

Jung, E. A. (2020). *I May Destroy You* Ending Explained. *Vulture*. www.vulture.com/2020/08/i-may-destroy-you-ending-explained-michaela-coel.html.

Killing Eve. (2018–2022). BBC.

King, S. (2014). Crime Fiction as World Literature. *Clues* 32(2), 8–19.

Kirino, N. (2003). *Out*. Vintage International.

Lerner, H. G. (1985). *The Dance of Anger: A Woman's Guide to Changing the Patterns of Intimate Relationships*. Harper & Row.

Lorde, A. (1981). The Uses of Anger. *Women's Studies Quarterly* 9(3), 7–10.

Manne, K. (2018). *Down Girl: The Logic of Misogyny*. Penguin.

Marsh, R. (2016). The Man Who Cut Off My Hair. In *The Complete Judith Lee Adventures*. Valancourt Books.

Martin, T. (2019). *Contemporary Drift: Genre, Historicism, and the Problem of the Present*. Columbia University Press.

Miller, E. V. (2018). "How Much Do You Want to Pay for This Beauty?": Domestic Noir and the Active Turn in Feminist Crime Fiction. In *Domestic Noir: The New Face of 21st Century Crime Fiction*, ed. L. Joyce and H. Sutton. Palgrave Macmillan, pp. 89–113.

Mina, D. (2009). *Still Midnight*. Back Bay Books.
Mina, D. (2011). *The End of the Wasp Season*. Back Bay Books.
Mina, D. (2014). *Gods and Beasts* and "A Conversation with Denise Mina." Back Bay Books.
Mina, D. (2023). Stepping Into Raymond Chandler's Shoes Showed Me the Power of Fiction. *New York Times*. August 26.
Moretti, F. (2000). Slaughterhouse of Literature. *Modern Language Quarterly* 61(1), 207–227.
Moretti, F. (2007). *Graphs, Maps, Trees*. Verso.
Munt, S. (1994). *Murder by the Book? Feminism and the Crime Novel*. Routledge.
Nakanishi, W. J. (2018). Contextualizing Crime: Kirino Natsuo's *Out*. *Japanese Language and Literature* 52(1), 127–144.
Nash, J. C. (2001). Practicing Love: Black Feminism, Love-Politics, and Post-Intersectionality. *Meridians* 11(2), 1–24.
Neely, B. (1992). *Blanche on the Lam*. Penguin.
Neely, B. (2000). *Blanche Passes Go*. Brash Books.
Ngai, S. (2005). *Ugly Feelings*. Harvard University Press.
Nickerson, C. R. (1998). *The Web of Iniquity: Early Detective Fiction by American Women*. Duke University Press.
Nussbaum, M. (2019). *Anger and Forgiveness: Resentment, Generosity, Justice*. Oxford University Press.
Paretsky, S. (1994). *Tunnel Vision*. Dell Publishing.
Paretsky, S. (2004). *Blacklist*. Signet.
Paretsky, S. (2007). *Writing in an Age of Silence*. Verso.
Paretsky, S. (2017). *Fallout*. William Morrow.
Paretsky, S. (2021). *Bitter Medicine*. William Morrow.
Pease, A. (2012). *Modernism, Feminism, and the Culture of Boredom*. Cambridge University Press.
Penny, L. (2018). *Bitch Doctrine: Essays for Dissenting Adults*. Bloomsbury.
Peters, F. (2018). The Literary Antecedents of Domestic Noir. In *Domestic Noir: The New Face of 21st Century Crime Fiction*, ed. L. Joyce and H. Sutton. Palgrave Macmillan, pp. 11–25.
Redhead, L. (2018). Teenage Kicks: Performance and Postfeminism in Domestic Noir. In *Domestic Noir: The New Face of 21st Century Crime Fiction*, ed. L. Joyce and H. Sutton. Palgrave Macmillan, pp. 115–135.
Reitz, C. (1999). Do We Need Another Hero? In *Multicultural Detective Fiction: Murder From the "Other" Side*, ed. A. J. Gosselin. Garland, pp. 213–233.
Reitz, C. (2015). Nancy Drew, *Dragon Tattoo*: Female Detective Fiction and the Ethics of Care. *Textus* 27(2), 19–46.

Robinson, B. S. (2023). Anger's Privilege. https://lareviewofbooks.org/article/angers-privilege/.

Rose, J. (2015). Corkscrew in the Neck. *London Review of Books*. www.lrb.co.uk/the-paper/v37/n17/jacqueline-rose/corkscrew-in-the-neck.

Schwarz, O. (2018). Calling out for Justice. https://ethics.org.au/calling-out-for-justice/.

Showalter, E. (1977). *A Literature of Their Own*. Princeton University Press.

Slung, M. (1975). *Crime on Her Mind*. Pantheon.

Sontag, S. (2001). Notes on "Camp." In *Against Interpretation and Other Essays*. Picador, pp. 275–92.

Surridge, L. (2005). *Bleak Houses: Marital Violence in Victorian Fiction*. Ohio University Press.

Sutton, H. (2018). Gone Genre: How the Academy Came Running and Discovered Nothing Was As It Seemed. In *Domestic Noir: The New Face of 21st Century Crime Fiction*, ed. L. Joyce and H. Sutton. Palgrave Macmillan, pp. 53–69.

Tatar, M. (2021). *The Heroine with 1,001 Faces*. Norton.

Todorov, T. (1977). *The Poetics of Prose*. Cornell University Press.

Traister, S. (2018). *Good and Mad: The Revolutionary Power of Women's Anger*. Simon & Schuster.

Vaughn, S. (2017). *Anatomy of a Scandal*. Emily Bestler Books.

Walton, S. (2015). *Guilty But Insane: Mind and Law in Golden Age Detective Fiction*. Oxford University Press.

Wasserman, R. (2016). What Does It Mean When We Call Women Girls? *LitHub*. https://lithub.com/what-does-it-mean-when-we-call-women-girls/.

Wilkinson, L. (2018). *American Spy*. Random House.

Williams, R. (1961). *The Long Revolution*. Columbia University Press.

Acknowledgments

While it might make sense to thank all those folks who've taught me first-hand about anger by pissing me off over the years, it is much more pleasing to celebrate all the wonderful students, colleagues, and friends who have shared my love of female-centered crime stories both in and out of the classroom. My undergraduate students at John Jay College of Criminal Justice in my "Crime Stories" and "Sisters in Crime" classes, and my grad students at the CUNY Graduate Center in my "Female Dicks" and "Madwomen" classes, have all been important interlocutors over the years. My CUNY colleagues, as well as my fellow crime fiction scholars around the world (some of whom serve on the *Clues* journal editorial board), have provided important feedback on these ideas over the years. Parts of these ideas were shared at the Research Society for Victorian Periodicals conference in 2021, the Captivating Criminality 8 conference in Bamberg in 2022, and the Democracy and Crime Fiction conference in Paris in 2023. I'm grateful to the organizers, especially Andrew Pepper, Benoit Tadie, and Dominique Jeannerod, and audience members in Nanterre for important suggestions. I appreciate the editors of the Elements in Crime Narratives series, Margot Douaihy, Catherine Ross Nickerson, and Henry Sutton, for inviting me to pull these long-simmering ideas together. Finally, thanks to my partner in crime and rompadre, Richard Haw, for the jolliest conversations about female anger and crime fiction that one could ever imagine.

Cambridge Elements

Crime Narratives

Margot Douaihy
Emerson College

Margot Douaihy, PhD, is an assistant professor at Emerson College in Boston. She is the author of *Scorched Grace* (Gillian Flynn Books/Zando, 2023), which was named one of the best crime novels of 2023 by *The New York Times*, *The Guardian*, and *CrimeReads*. Her recent scholarship includes the "Beat the Clock: Queer Temporality and Disrupting Chrononormativity in Crime Fiction," a NeMLA 2024 paper.

Catherine Nickerson
Emory College of Arts and Sciences

Catherine Ross Nickerson is the author of *The Web of Iniquity: Early Detective Fiction by American Women* (Duke University Press, 1999), which was nominated for an Edgar Award by the Mystery Writers of America. She is the editor of *The Cambridge Companion to American Crime Fiction* (2010), as well as two volumes of reprinted novels by Anna Katharine Green and Metta Fuller Victor (Duke University Press).

Henry Sutton
University of East Anglia

Henry Sutton, SFHEA, is Professor of Creative Writing and Crime Fiction at the University of East Anglia. He is the author of fifteen novels, including two crime fiction series. His is also the author of the *Crafting Crime Fiction* (Manchester University Press, 2023), and the co-editor of *Domestic Noir: The New Face of 21st Century Crime Fiction* (Palgrave Macmillan, 2018).

Advisory Board

William Black, *Johns Hopkins University*
Christopher Breu, *Illinois State University*
Cathy Cole, *Liverpool John Moores University and University of Wollongong*
Stacy Gillis, *Newcastle University*
Femi Kayode, *Author (Namibia)*
Andrew Pepper, *Belfast University*
Barbara Pezzotti, *Monash University*
Richie Narvaez, *Fashion Institute of Technology*
Clare Rolens, *Palomar College*
Shampa Roy, *University of Delhi*
David Schmid, *University of Buffalo*
Samantha Walton, *Bath Spa University*
Aliki Varvogli, *University of Dundee*

About the Series

Publishing groundbreaking research from scholars and practitioners of crime writing in its many dynamic and evolving forms, this series examines and re-examines crime narratives as a global genre which began on the premise of entertainment, but quickly evolved to probe pressing political and sociological concerns, along with the human condition.

Cambridge Elements

Crime Narratives

Elements in the Series

Forensic Crime Fiction
Aliki Varvogli

Female Anger in Crime Fiction
Caroline Reitz

A full series listing is available at: www.cambridge.org/ECNA

For EU product safety concerns, contact us at Calle de José Abascal, 56–1°, 28003 Madrid, Spain or eugpsr@cambridge.org.

www.ingramcontent.com/pod-product-compliance
Lightning Source LLC
LaVergne TN
LVHW020351260326
834688LV00045B/1668